SEED LIFE

Engaging Every Person with a Kingdom Mindset

Justin R. Jones

with Sherrill Auker

To my Sister:
Who, for my whole life, has faithfully demonstrated how
to live a Seed Life and encouraged me to do the same

To my Youth Pastors growing up:
Who demonstrated for me how to live with grace and
patience in ministry

To the lay leaders of Eastern Hills Church:
You are a living demonstration of Seed Life

ACKNOWLEDGMENTS

A big thank you to:

- Shawn King and Corey Nieman for their partnership in ministry
- To my wife, Janelle Jones, for her loving support
- Dawn Waggoner, Peggy Farrington, Danielle King, Joni Canastraro, and others who helped get the book ready for publishing
- All those who allowed us to use their story

CONTENTS

INTRODUCTION

Do you ever have moments where you feel in over your head? I had one of those experiences when I was on a trip with my youth group in high school. We had traveled to a conference in Chicago that focused on evangelism: sharing the Good News of the Gospel with people. I really wanted people to know about Jesus (which is why I came to the conference in the first place), but I was also terrified. You see, this was not just a typical "sit-and-we'll-teach-you" kind of conference. At certain times throughout the week we were dropped off on the streets of Chicago to share the Gospel with random strangers.

Growing up, I was a shy child who was not always gifted at small talk. I could have deep conversations with someone I knew in a heartbeat, but small talk did not really make sense to me. It was hard for me to come up with interesting things to talk about. So the idea of engaging strangers on the street was daunting enough as it was. But then, on top of that, the expectation was that we would be interacting with these strangers in order to share with them the most important news that could ever be shared. Talk about overwhelming! This Good News we were supposed to share had eternal consequences for their souls. There was this fear in me that if I did not get this interaction right I was going to be jeopardizing their eternal destiny.

So there I stood, in the Rainbow district of Chicago, with a small group of students who were supposed to strike up conversations with people. Teams of students had been sent all around the city and this was our area. One conversation after another I tried my best. I wanted to get this right. But I felt like I was failing; failing the person I was talking to, the expectations of the conference organizers, and ultimately, God.

Have you ever felt this way about sharing the Gospel with people? A deep, overwhelming sense of failure? Sometimes this sense of failure comes when we try to share the Gospel with people and it does not turn out the way we hoped. Other times we feel like a failure because we know we should be sharing the Gospel with people, but we do not invest any energy into doing it.

I have asked people over the past several months the question, "What keeps you from sharing the Gospel with people?" The overwhelming response is fear. And although this fear can take many forms I think the primary form many of us feel is the fear of failure. We are haunted by the question, "What if I do it wrong?" This was my greatest question when I was in Chicago.

What should we do about this fear so many of us feel? The reality is that the Church's mission and every Christian's primary objective is to share the Good News of Jesus. And yet, the majority of Christians seem to have a deep struggle in their souls about whether they can actually do it. It leaves us in a place where the church is only a shadow of what it was meant to be and countless people leave this planet daily without hearing the Good News of salvation through Jesus Christ.

As I pondered how to respond to this question, it became obvious to me that an answer would only come by understanding evangelism in its greater context. You see, I am thankful for the conference I attended in Chicago years ago. I was able to learn a lot about myself, about evangelism, and about people through the experiences I had there. But it would have been easy to come away from that experience with a skewed view of evangelism; a view of evangelism that many other people might share.

In this skewed view of evangelism, we are convinced that evangelism is an event instead of a process. We are convinced that good evangelism happens through people who are eloquent, and if you do not have a way with words you should not even try. We are convinced that we have to know so much information to do evangelism correctly because evangelism means intellectually arguing people into salvation. We are convinced evangelism is only successful if there is an immediate and absolute response to our call for someone to receive the Gospel.

Personally, we are convinced that we are not fully equipped for evangelism so the best we can do is get our friends and family to "professional" Christians, like pastors, who can share the Good News correctly. Ultimately, we are convinced that evangelism is important, but the best we can hope to do is support other people, usually "professional" Christians, in their evangelism efforts.

Recently, I have been intrigued by the exploits of a climber named Alex Honnold. He practices a form of climbing called "free soloing." To do a free solo climb means you climb a mountain or sheer cliff without the aid of ropes or any safety gear. You are literally climbing up a rock wall with no support except for chalk and some climbing shoes. If you place your hand or foot in the wrong position, if you slip on a wet rock, if a bird flies up and distracts you, or if you simply lose focus for a second, you will die.

Recently, Alex completed a free solo climb of El Capitan, considered one of the most difficult climbs for regular climbers with climbing gear. The sheer rock wall rises three thousand feet above Yosemite National Park. Other expert climbers usually take several days to climb El Capitan and use ropes and harnesses and all kinds of safety equipment. But for Alex, he literally walked up to the wall and started climbing. It took him approximately four hours, but in the end he conquered El Capitan.[1]

Now, I am not a climber. Climbing up on the roof of my house gives me weak knees. So why am I so interested in Alex's story? Because I love to witness the mastery of something. Alex did not just wake up one morning, decide to climb one of the most difficult mountains in the world, and go do it. It took him years of mental, physical, and emotional preparation.

Yet, as I watch him, despite my understanding of his preparation, my constant thought still is, "I could never do that." I am not strong enough, brave enough, or crazy enough to take the steps he is taking. If I was to face that rock wall, I would see it as an insurmountable hurdle and set up camp at the bottom of the mountain (for the rest of my life if necessary) so I would not have to climb it.

I believe this is the way many of us view the process of evangelism. We think pastors, missionaries, evangelists, and "professional Christians" are like Alex. We hear stories about them sharing the Gospel with people resulting in many starting a relationship with Jesus. We even hear them tell stories of ministering to people who radically broke free from addictions and sin issues that were pervasive in their life. We are excited for them and want to support them any way we can, but to think we could do that same thing immediately strikes fear into our hearts. "We will stay camped out at the base of the mountain and cheer them on" we say to ourselves, because we will never have enough knowledge, enough wisdom, enough eloquence with words, or a strong enough faith to lead someone into a relationship with Jesus.

But what if we have gotten evangelism all wrong? What if it is not about having enough knowledge, wisdom, words, or faith to save someone? What if we have applied our own cultural ideas to the ways of Jesus and it is holding us back from truly living a fruitful Christian life? What if evangelism is not primarily a "science" to be studied, but instead it is the natural outflow of the Christian life Jesus talks about? Ultimately, what if Jesus' teachings on evangelism are far simpler and yet more profound than our way of thinking about evangelism?

These are the questions I hope to tackle in this book. In order to examine these questions, I would like to take us back to the original mission we were all given at the very beginning of creation: gardening. In Genesis 2:8 it says, "Now the Lord God had planted a garden in the east, in Eden; and there he put the man he had formed." Several verses later in Genesis 2:15 it says of Adam, "The Lord God took the man and put him in the Garden of Eden to work it and take care of it."[2] The first task assigned to the first humans ever created was to care for a garden.

I do not think it is any mistake, then, that when Jesus comes declaring the Kingdom of God many of His stories and parables revolve around gardening or farming practices. It also makes sense because the people of Jesus' time knew what it meant to produce food. There were no supermarkets. There was no fast food. People were not disconnected from the source of their food like we often are today. In fact, for most of human history, the reality of caring for and producing your own food was a nearly universal fact of human existence. So, when Jesus came telling stories and parables about soils, seeds, and harvests, people would have had a tangible understanding of what He meant.

In the past century or so, however, there has been a radical transformation of how we interact with our food. This universal and ancient understanding of what it meant to be involved in the cultivating process has been replaced with an almost magical place called "the grocery store." So few of us even know how the plants and animals we eat are grown.

As far back as the 1980's there was a recognition of the major shift in the amount of the American population who were farmers. In a 1988 New York Times Article entitled "Farm Population Lowest since 1850's," they estimated that only about 2 percent of the United States population were farmers at the time.[3] The article goes on to say that in the 1850's, it is estimated that about 64 percent of the nation's work force were farmers.

If so few of our population actually work to produce the plants and animals that feed us on a regular basis, it means most of us can live our whole lives with no idea of how seeds and plants grow. This is how I lived most of my life. I never remember growing a single plant in my entire life until my mid-twenties. I ate many different kinds of foods, but I could not tell you what kind of plant a tomato grew on, whether potatoes actually even came from a plant, or that *rocket* is actually a lettuce green and not just a vehicle that sends people into space.

After I got married, growing plants was a little more on my radar since my wife had some interest. Then, one year I spent time talking to my sister-in-law, Sherrill, about growing vegetables. She is an agricultural missionary in Zambia and the Democratic Republic of Congo, specializing in helping people grow their own food in order to provide for their family and community. (She has written several Seed Life spotlights that are interspersed throughout this book, so you will get to know more about her ministry.)

In talking with her several years ago, an interest was sparked in me to learn more about how plants grow. I got a book about it and started reading. Then I asked our landlord at the time if I could start a small garden in the backyard of our apartment.

At the time I would have been ecstatic to simply have a couple plants grow successfully and get some food out of them by the end of the summer. I thought this would be a fun little experiment that probably would not last. Thankfully, we did get some good food out of that first small garden we made. But something much deeper happened to me that I did not anticipate. In the process of working the soil, sowing the seeds, pulling the weeds, watering the plants, and harvesting the food I started to experience some of the parables of Jesus for the first time.

I would be breaking up the soil and a Scripture about hard-heartedness would pop into my mind. I would watch seeds I had planted grow into productive plants and I would experience the joy Jesus must have been pointing to when He talked about seeds planted in good soil producing a crop. Pulling out deep roots of weeds would get me thinking about how Scripture speaks about dealing with roots of bitterness that can develop in our souls.

Since those early years, my wife and I have grown more and more of our own food, and there are many aspects of it we enjoy. But the greatest thing that excites me is the more I learn about how God has organized the natural world, the more insight I seem to get into what God wants to do in the world spiritually through His Kingdom. Primarily, I think there is a reason God uses so many pictures of gardening and farming to speak about evangelism in Scripture, which is why I decided to call this book "Seed Life."

Throughout the book I will be using these words as a noun, "seed-life," and also as a verb, to "seed life." I believe if we truly understand what Jesus meant when He spoke about the Kingdom of God, and if we follow the instructions we find within many of the Gospel parables, we will discover a different picture of what evangelism truly is. I hope to explain why I believe Jesus' commands for evangelism simply entail "engaging every person with a kingdom mindset." I will be using the picture of continually sowing seeds or having a "seed-life" as the backdrop to explain this.

Now, you may be thinking, "I know nothing about plants or growing food and I really don't care to learn, so maybe this book isn't for me." Although I really enjoy growing food and have learned so much from the process, I am not writing a book to persuade you to garden. I will tell stories from my experiences simply to better explain some of the statements of Jesus, but this is NOT a gardening book. This is a book that uses gardening and farming to expound on some deep spiritual truths. As Joel Salatin says in his book *The Marvelous Pigness of*

Pigs, "...creation is an object lesson of spiritual truth. Just like object lessons for children point them to biblical principles, so the physical universe is supposed to point us to God."[4] Please do not let the object lesson and your agreement or disagreement about the object lesson become your sole focus in this book. The intention is to use creation to point us to deep spiritual truths about evangelism.

More importantly, you might be thinking, "He says this book is about evangelism and honestly I am just trying to focus on getting my own life together. Anytime I hear a pastor or teacher talk about sharing the Gospel with others it only brings me more guilt about how my life is messed up. I am not sure I can handle another message telling me I am not doing things right." Just like the example of comparing ourselves to Alex Honnolt earlier, we feel like we will never succeed so why even try?

To you, I would just say that I understand what you are feeling, but I hope you would consider reading a little further into the book. Yes, this book will focus on evangelism, but I think part of the reason we get wrong ideas about evangelism in the first place is because we have taken it out of its greater context – the Kingdom of God. My hope is that through this book you would discover not only a way to better think about evangelism, but a better context to understand your whole life with God.

So I invite you into this journey with me to discover what it means to have a "seed-life." I believe the best way to read something or study something is to do it in community. When others around you are reading it as well, it gives context for conversation, accountability, and clarity. So before you dive in, take a second to consider who you want to invite to go on this journey as well. Maybe it's a family member, a small group, or a friend you work with. At the end of every chapter there are reading questions and application questions I hope will be helpful conversation starters as you walk together.

1
A NEW PICTURE OF
THE KINGDOM OF GOD

Clanging, galloping, loud cheers, clashing steel, dust, the smell of meat: these are the sounds and smells of a vague memory I have from a childhood trip. We were on a vacation as a family and decided to go to "Medieval Times." If you have never been there, imagine walking back into the times of knights and castles. You are ushered into stadium seating of sorts with a wooden table in front of you. "Medieval" food is served: large pieces of meat that you eat with your hands and other assorted food items served on metal plates.

Then the real show begins. In front of you is a large arena. Different knights are introduced each riding out on his faithful steed. First, the black knight, then the green knight, then the white knight, and on it goes. You are to cheer for one of the knights as they battle each other in medieval sport. Perhaps your knight continues on through the gauntlet, or if great misfortune occurs and he cannot withstand the "valiant battles" he is knocked out of the contest.

I remember my young mind being enthralled with the whole experience. Obviously, it was all just simply entertainment, but the experience seemed so close to the real thing. And for a young boy, there was something enchanting about the idea of being a medieval knight battling with the forces of evil to stand for what is right.

Maybe you are not like me, but when I think about the word "kingdom" it is these sorts of pictures that come to mind: castles, battles, knights, swords. I picture King Arthur and the Knights of the Round Table, noble steeds galloping across open fields, kings on their thrones with a court of people around them. When I think about these things, I have a strange sense of nostalgia. Maybe it is the mysterious and dream-like nature of it all. Maybe it is all the books I read and Disney movies I watched growing up that had these themes. Maybe it is a yearning to go back to a day when themes like chivalry and honor seemed to come through in the stories.

Whatever the case, we must confront our own understanding of the word "kingdom" before we go any further in this book. As I said earlier, I believe understanding Jesus' meaning behind the "Kingdom of God" will help illuminate how we are to go about sharing the Gospel. But if we are to effectively understand Jesus' meaning of the words "kingdom of God" we must confront our own understanding of the word "kingdom" first.

You see, when I hear the "Kingdom of God" my mind immediately pictures Jesus seated on a throne in royal dress sending out His knights on their galloping horses to fight spiritual battles and destroy the enemy. Now, not all of this is far off from what the Bible talks about. In Isaiah 6, we hear about a vision that Isaiah experiences. In this vision, God is sitting on His throne and the description of Him as King is more majestic and awe-inspiring than any medieval tale that could be told. Around God's throne are resplendent angels singing songs of glory to Him.

We should not shy away at all from the reality that God, the King, is sovereign over all things. In fact, the primary meaning of the "Kingdom of God" in Scripture has to do with His reign and control over all things. As R.T. France says, "The phrase 'the kingdom of God' therefore points not to a specific situation or event, but to 'God in control', with all the breadth of meaning that that phrase could cover. Attempts to *define* 'the kingdom of God' inevitably restrict this breadth, and so fail to do justice to the variety of its usage in the Gospels."[5] God is the rightful ruler of all things and when we come into relationship with Him and join His Kingdom, we get to participate in His work to bring all things under His Kingdom authority.

I am not saying we should deny this truth about the Kingdom of God, but I believe we need to expand our idea of what is meant by "God in control." You see, my concern is we might interpret these kingdom references in Scripture solely by our ideas of medieval kingdoms. When we do that, we tend to focus all of our attention on battles, noble knights, and dangerous dragons or monsters.

There are two main results from only interpreting the Kingdom this way. First, some people think the idea of the Kingdom of God is so far off and distant that it does not really apply to their life today. They think it was a nice way for people to talk about God in history, but those spiritual realities (at least interpreted in that way) are not as applicable today.

The second way people may skew their perspective on the Kingdom is to think the only way they can participate in the Kingdom is to be that "noble knight" who goes out to face the "monster" and does "battle" with people who are stuck in the kingdom of darkness. Again, this is not completely wrong. In different scriptures, the devil is referenced as a serpent and lion seeking those he can destroy. Also, we are called to put on our armor to stand in battle against the enemy in Ephesians 6.

The problem is that someone who is completely focused on this way of interpreting the Kingdom will often think about sharing the Gospel this way as well. They will feel as though they have an important position of power sent out to do God's work and will expect opposition and battles as they go out to share the Gospel. They have prepared and are ready to do battle with their actions, their words, and their lives. They believe if they face opposition it is a demonstration that their course is correct.

Don't get me wrong. There are times when we are going to be called by God to stand up and speak about Him in the midst of hostile environments. But the opposition these people face is often self-induced. They have taken a hostile tone to people and those people have responded in kind.

Someone who believes this is their mission may stand on a street corner shouting and using a sign to decry a particular sin or way of living. Or another person with this mindset may purposely start intellectual battles with their friends who do not know Jesus yet in the hopes of showing them that their arguments are completely faulty. Still others may post jarring statements on social media in the hope of unsettling their friends. Some may judge the sin of their friends who do not know Jesus with the mindset that they have to know they are offending God.

The problem with all of these cases is that in the course of people trying to share the Gospel they have forgotten the most important ingredient: love. 1 Corinthians 13:1-3 says:

If I speak in the tongues of men or of angels, but do not have love, I am only a resounding gong or a clanging cymbal. If I have the gift of prophecy and can fathom all mysteries and all knowledge, and if I have a faith that can move mountains, but do not have love, I am nothing. If I give all I possess to the poor and give over my body to hardship that I may boast, but do not have love, I gain nothing.[6]

I admire the heart of many of these people because in their mind they are fighting the battle of God to save souls. The sad thing to me is they have missed the whole point of the Gospel. If we are not showing love in the way we reach out to others, then are we truly sharing the Gospel?

Many people in this camp could argue that they are loving people by trying to save them. But their understanding of how to save souls has been fueled by an understanding of the Kingdom that is only partially complete. The problem of only seeing this medieval picture of the Kingdom is that it primarily focuses on the mechanisms of winning souls and boils evangelism down to an oppositional short-term event that must be won. This perspective ignores other elements of Jesus' teaching, which would point toward evangelism as a relational long-term process demanding our cultivation of faithful love and care.

ANOTHER PICTURE OF THE KINGDOM

How would it change our perspective if we also interpreted the Kingdom through a different picture used throughout Scripture: the picture of a garden? Remember we said in the introduction that when God first created all things He started with a garden. He placed Adam and Eve there and established a place for them to flourish and live with Him.

Then something truly egregious happened: the very ones He planted in the garden to flourish decided to turn their backs on Him by sinning. In Genesis 3 they are deceived by the serpent and then choose to take fruit from the tree that God forbid them to eat from. In this action the seed of death was sown into the garden. In Romans 7:5 Paul illustrates the nature of sin that was a result of this action when he says, "For when we were in the realm of the flesh, the sinful passions aroused by the law were at work in us, so that we bore fruit for death."[7] God had told Adam and Eve in Genesis 2:16-17, "...You are free to eat from any tree in the garden; but you must not eat from the tree of the knowledge of good and evil, for when you eat from it you will certainly die."[8] When they chose to go against God's command, a seed was sown in the garden of Eden that would ultimately bear the fruit of death: both physical and spiritual death in them and us.

Now, remember, if we are using the term "Kingdom of God" then it describes God's great dominion and control over all things. Despite this seed of death being sown in the garden of Eden it was still His garden. He had the full right to take that garden and completely uproot everything in it and start again.

Recently, I went with some friends to check out a house that was in foreclosure. When we opened the door you could tell by the stench alone that this house was going to be hard to redeem. As we ventured inside and observed the trash, dilapidated furniture, and shaky structure of the building, the comment was made that it would be better to tear down the whole house and start again then try to redeem it.

The same could have been true for God. He could have looked at His garden and decided that it would be better to uproot everything and start again and He would have had every right to do just that. But Jesus tells a parable that gives us some insight into why He chose a different way. This parable is found in Matthew 13 and it is called the "Parable of the Weeds." In it he says:

> *The kingdom of Heaven is like a man who sowed good seed in his field. But while everyone was sleeping, his enemy came and sowed weeds among the wheat, and went away. When the wheat sprouted and formed heads, then the weeds also appeared.*[9]

The parable goes on to say that the owner's servants came to him and asked if he wanted them to pull up the weeds. The owner says not to uproot the weeds because it may uproot the wheat growing with them. Instead, he says in Matthew 13:30, "Let both grow together until the harvest. At that time I will tell the harvesters: First collect the weeds and tie them in bundles to be burned; then gather the wheat and bring it into my barn."[10]

The first thing this parable tells us is the heart of God in relation to the garden. Although He is more than able and sometimes willing to bring about His justice in His Kingdom by uprooting and destroying, He often finds far more creative ways to bring about His loving justice than to simply destroy. His justice is not arbitrary and destructive; it is done with love.

It reminds me of my grandfather. He is one of the most kind, humble, and generous men I have ever met. I have also been told he was one of the best disciplinarians when my mom and my uncle were growing up. One of the stories told about him begins one day when my mom and uncle were picking on each other over and over again, trying to accuse each other about something. They wanted the other one to get punished. So instead of disciplining them both, my grandfather took off his belt and gave it to my mom. He said something to the effect of, "If you are so frustrated with each other, then go ahead and discipline each other."

Now, you might be thinking, "Was he crazy?", based on your family dynamics. You might be thinking that if someone gave you a belt to discipline your sibling with you would have smiled with glee and started running after them. But he knew his kids and he knew that it would teach them something. They both started crying, lightly tapped each other with the belt, and they never tried to accuse each other in the same way again. My grandfather knew they would learn a deeper lesson if he creatively brought about his justice than if he would have simply released his wrath.

In a similar way, one of the things the parable of the weeds alludes to is the patience and creative nature of our God. He is not arbitrary in His justice, even though He has complete and supreme control, because He loves us.

Another thing the parable alludes to is the creative way God decided to redeem His garden. Later on in Matthew 13, Jesus interprets the parable for His disciples. He defines the different parts of the parable by saying in Matthew 13:37-39, "The one who sowed the good seed is the Son of Man. The field is the world, and the good seed stands for the people of the kingdom. The weeds are the people of the evil one, and the enemy who sows them is the devil. The harvest is the end of the age, and the harvesters are angels."[11]

Jesus, through this parable, is describing the end of the age or end of time. The parable is pointing to the fact that ultimate justice will not be dealt out until He comes back and His angels will "weed out of his kingdom everything that causes sin and all who do evil."[12] But it also describes the plan that was enacted to redeem the world. First, this parable says the Son of Man, or Jesus, was the one who sowed good seed. Jesus was key in God the Father's plan of redemption. God the Father chose to use His Son in order to sow redemption into His "garden."

How did this happen? In John 12:23-24, Jesus says, "The hour has come for the Son of Man to be glorified. Very truly I tell you, unless a kernel of wheat falls to the ground and dies, it remains only a single seed. But if it dies, it produces many seeds."[13] The whole plan of redemption, the point of the Gospel, is the death and resurrection of Jesus Christ. We as people were incapable of dealing with the seed of death ourselves. We deserved destruction because we were wrapped up with the weeds of destruction and death. But as it says in Romans 5:8, "…God demonstrates his own love for us in this: while we were still sinners, Christ died for us."[14] If you do not understand the supreme importance of the death and resurrection of Jesus in the Gospel message then I encourage you to read my other book, *ENGAGE: How to Know God.*

But what Jesus is declaring in John 12 is the outcome of His death and resurrection. He is saying to His disciples, "I have to die, because the only way the seed of life is going to spread throughout this world and bring redemption is through My death and resurrection." Joel Salatin is a Christian farmer, teacher, and author who writes on the intersection between faith and creation. He says this about the spiritual importance of seeds in creation: "He's (God) obviously interested in succession and procreation because that's the whole plan of evangelism and spreading the good news of the gospel. The New Testament is all about successful replication. Jesus making disciples is a case in point."[15]

The process of a seed being sown, the seed "dying" so it can sprout into life, the plant growing until it bears fruit, then the plant dropping its fruit to spread its seed, is the pattern of creation. Salatin would contend that God has put into creation echoes of His spiritual Kingdom, so when we observe the process of a seed we should consider its spiritual implications.

JESUS SEEDING LIFE

So let's consider this different picture of the Kingdom in its entirety. First, God the Father is like a gardener. In John 15:1, Jesus says, "I am the true vine, and my father is the gardener."[16] God the Father established a good garden, the garden of Eden, that was meant to flourish. The enemy, Satan, came in and tempted Adam and Eve to sin. In their choice to sin, the seed of death was sown into the garden. Imagine with me a gorgeous garden that had weed seeds blown into it and is now covered with aggressive and destructive weeds.

God the Father had the right to uproot the entire garden and start again with good seed. But instead of completely uprooting everything and destroying the good with the bad, He had a longer view in mind. He decides to send His Son, Jesus, who was already described in John 15 as the true vine. Imagine with me that God the Father plants the vine in the middle of this garden that is overgrown with weeds.

Now, the vine was powerful and could have simply covered the weeds, but instead the vine, Jesus, dies in order to produce more good seed in the garden. Remember John

12:24, "Very truly I tell you, unless a kernel of wheat falls to the ground and dies, it remains only a single seed. But if it dies, it produces many seeds."[17] Through Jesus' death and resurrection, He in turn is seeding life into any good soil He finds, and the plants that grow from those seeds will in turn produce good seed, which will seed life into other good soil, until all good soil in the whole garden is redeemed.

And here is where the picture gets really exciting. Guess who those plants are that grow from Jesus seeding life? They are anyone who has surrendered their life to God and are in a relationship with Him. You and me. Are you seeing the picture?

So often we are hindered from sharing the Gospel with other people because we feel so removed from the process. We say, "I really want to let my family and friends and neighbors know about Jesus, but it is only God that can save people." And if you say this, you would certainly be right. Only God can truly draw people toward Himself, forgive their sins, and transform their life. But how do you think He goes about doing that? Through us!

The point is, if we embrace this picture of the Kingdom of God as a garden, then we can understand the truth that, however strange and unbelievable it might be, God has chosen you and I to be part of His redeeming process for the world. Not only has He chosen us, but in fact, evangelism or seeding life as He did is not some magical process only certain people like "professional Christians" have access to. It is simply the natural outflow of someone who is truly following Jesus. When God plants good seed into the soil of our heart and we grow into the plant God intends, we will by very nature seed life into the hearts of others. As it says in 1 Corinthians 3:5-9:

What, after all, is Apollos? And what is Paul? Only servants, through whom you came to believe – as the Lord has assigned each his task. I planted the seed, Apollos watered it, but God has been making it grow. So neither the one who plants nor the one who waters is anything, but only God, who makes things grow. The one who plants and the one who waters have one purpose, and they will each be rewarded according to their own labor. For we are God's co-workers in God's service; you are God's field, God's building.[18]

The people of Corinth were having squabbles about who followed the teaching of Apollos and who followed the teaching of Paul. Paul responds by saying some incredible things.

First, he takes the pressure off of us. Remember, I said seeding life or evangelizing should be a natural outworking of our lives if we know Jesus. Some of you probably freaked out and started putting all kinds of pressure on yourself saying things like, "I need to go out and save someone right now" or "I am probably a terrible Christian because evangelism feels uncomfortable sometimes." Paul alleviates the pressure to some extent by reminding us that those of us who lead people *to* God do not matter nearly as much *as* God, because He is the one that makes things grow.

If I went out in my garden or a farmer went out in their field and sowed seed, but God decided to stop making seeds act like seeds and produce life there would be nothing in our soil. We are 100% dependent on God producing life through a seed in the ground and we are 100% dependent on God producing life in someone else. Life is not produced in someone else by how well we say things or how powerfully we lead a worship service or how generous we are, although all these are good things. We can do all of these to the best of our ability and it is still 100% dependent on God to produce life in someone else.

You might say, "then what is the point? If it depends 100% on God to produce life in someone else, then why does it matter what I do?" Paul addresses this too. He says those who plant and those who water have a purpose in the process. They have each been given a task to live out in regards to evangelism. Then he says an incredible statement in verse 9, "For we are God's co-workers…"[19] Do you hear that? We are God's co-workers.

Even though God would not need us to do so, He has chosen that we would be His co-workers in the redemption of the world. He has chosen to put gifts and purposes inside each one of us that would be used to seed life into other people so He could redeem the world. When we surrender our lives to Jesus Christ and accept His seed of life into our hearts, we become part of His Kingdom work. As the Bible says in Revelation 1:6, "And [He] has made us to be a kingdom and priests to serve his God and Father – to him be glory and power for ever and ever! Amen."[20]

And as His coworker, we are not being tasked with saving the whole world. We have been given a place and a circle of influence in the Kingdom of God. Just like a seed is planted in a particular place and the resulting plant has the ability to influence the area directly around it, so we are planted in the Kingdom of God and are tasked with seeding life in the places we are planted. Sometimes we are stunted from sharing the Gospel at all because we believe sharing the Gospel or evangelizing means constantly walking up to random people and asking them if they love Jesus. There may be an occasion where God asks you to do something like that, but in general, God has planted you among your family, friends, coworkers, neighborhood, and areas of influence for a reason. If we stop feeling the need to save the whole world, we may become better at reaching the circle of influence where God has planted us.

As we each take our places in God's redeeming work, that picture of a garden overgrown with weeds will start to change. Over time, as more and more good seed is planted into good soil, we will start to see God's "Kingdom come" and "will be done on earth as it is in heaven."[21] Our families, friends, churches, neighborhoods, community organizations, schools, businesses, and regions will start to be transformed by the love of God. And His Kingdom will start to become more evident on earth and choke out the seed of death present in the world.

I planted a small garden several years ago when we moved into our new house. The first year I planted some of the regular things you might find in a garden like tomatoes, lettuce, and peas. It was really good soil and the plants took off, especially the tomatoes. I tore everything out at the end of the season and started planning out the next season's crops.

In the next season I carefully planted a whole assortment of different seeds in the bed. Imagine my surprise when many seedlings I did not plant started to germinate and crowded out what I had intentionally planted. As I looked closer, I realized that the tomatoes from the previous year had left so much viable seed in that small garden that I had dozens of volunteer tomatoes growing without me intentionally planting them.

The following season the same thing happened but worse. I had so many volunteer tomatoes that almost everything else in the garden bed struggled to grow because they were getting choked out by the tremendous amount of tomatoes.

Now, imagine my garden bed as the Kingdom of God. As we accept the good seed of the Gospel from Jesus and live out our lives faithfully growing with Him and producing fruit, God will start to change the landscape around us. And it all starts as we stop resisting the seed-life He has planted within us.

The rest of this book will seek to explore how this natural process of seeding life happens and how we can make sure we are participating in God's plan of redemption, but I hope you understand the enormity of these truths. If we do not understand the very foundation of what the Kingdom of God is and the pattern God has established to save the world, we will have a hard time living it out.

I hope you realize how exciting it is to be called to this mission. You see, if coming to church and trying to live out Jesus' commands is simply a religious duty to you, then you would never imagine in your wildest dreams that God could use you to seed life in other people. You would never feel qualified and honestly you would probably never be excited enough to share your faith with someone else because it is more of a burden to you than a joy.

However, if you have surrendered your life to Jesus and are in a transforming relationship with Him, then understand the position you are in: you are now living with the Holy Spirit of God within you. He can empower and awaken you to particular gifts and abilities and purposes that you alone have been given to reach your circle of influence. You have been planted in a region or circle of influence within which you have been given the momentous task of seeding Kingdom life. This means it is not your pastor's job to share the Gospel with your circle of influence. *You* actually have your own marching orders, just like your pastor does. How exciting is that!

When we finally start to engage other people with a Kingdom mindset our whole worldview changes. Faith goes from dull and boring to exciting and thrilling. We go from barely being able to conquer sin to seeing miraculous things happen in our lives and the lives of people around us. We are pushed into a deeper and more satisfying relationship with God because we are no longer merely learning about God intellectually, but we are experiencing actual Kingdom work. And we can give all the glory back to God in the end because He is the one who has provided life throughout the whole process. We have simply been faithful to seed life by engaging every person we come in contact with, with a Kingdom mindset.

I remember when my friend, Julian, had this happen in his faith. I met Julian at college when he became a resident in the dorm where I was a leader. He was already a follower of Jesus and a really nice guy, but in college I saw him flourish into the amazing Kingdom worker he is today. He and I spent a lot of time together, talking about God's Word, praying together, confessing sin to one another, and sharing testimonies. God started to break down some walls in Julian and allowed him to fully embrace the Kingdom purposes he had been designed for.

In my later years of college, I watched as the intensity and excitement with which Julian followed God changed. He became more focused and disciplined in his faith. He took more risks and steps of faith. As he dated the woman who is now his wife, he had a newfound Kingdom mindset. As he embraced people around him, he had a newfound Kingdom mindset. Whether it was by his words or his actions, he was starting to be used tremendously to help seed life into everyone around him.

After college, Julian got married and moved to southern Indiana where he is a public school teacher. He could have lived the typical life for someone like him: a good Christian guy attending church consistently, with a pleasant wife and kids, and a nice house, faithfully teaching his students but being quiet about his faith as he goes about his business. But he discovered long ago that Kingdom life and his role to seed life is much more than just the standard, average, "nice" life. He has a mission, a circle of influence, and a great God who can bring life out of darkness.

Because of this, Julian did not just buy any old house; he bought a house right next to the school. Not only that, but he has taken his role to seed life as a teacher seriously. He has obtained grants for the school to build an outdoor garden, an outdoor interactive park, and other resources outside of the school. His intention is to provide better spaces for him to invest in his students and community and to provide spaces for better relationships to take place.

Julian and his wife started opening their home to foreign exchange students and sharing the Good News of Jesus with them, even while starting a family of their own. He has not only attended his church faithfully but has served in various capacities within the church. They have intentionally used their home during holidays and other times to host parties or bless people so they can know the love of Jesus. He has done all of this while continuing to encourage the growth of faith in his wife and kids.

When I talk to him, do you think he feels as though life is boring and dull? Not at all! He is one of the most exciting and encouraging people I talk to, always giving glory to God for the blessings he has received.

Now, I can hear some of you saying, "Well, that is nice for Julian, but he must be a super-Christian. There is no way my life could be that intense for the Kingdom of God." But Julian would be the first to say he is just a normal guy. There is nothing in and of himself that has caused him to have such an impact. It is simply because Julian got serious about his role in the Kingdom of God that God is now using his life to such an extent.

In the rest of the book we will talk more specifically about the way that this seed life is lived out in us. But before we move on we must ask ourselves, "What is keeping us from living a life like Julian?" Is it a lack of understanding, a lack of knowledge? Is it sin and selfishness? Is it that you have never truly experienced the grace of God and are simply living out a "religious life"?

Before you move on, take a moment to think through these questions.

REFLECTION QUESTIONS

1. If we think about the Kingdom of God as some distant, ethereal idea we may not take seriously the urgent need for evangelism. Do you feel like you have a clear and urgent picture of evangelism?

2. If we only have a medieval picture of the Kingdom it can make us abrasive in our evangelism. Have you or someone you've known tried to evangelize this way? How did it turn out?

3. What stood out to you the most about considering the Kingdom of God as a garden?

4. Julian was used as an example of someone who discovered a fruitful Kingdom life. What is keeping you from living this kind of life with Jesus?

5. Did anything else stand out to you from this chapter?

APPLICATION

1. JOURNAL – Even if you are not someone who journals often, take some time to write down your thoughts on the Kingdom of God before we go further in the book. Write down your reaction to what this chapter talked about. Also, write down three people in your life you know are not in a relationship with Jesus. These people will be the ones you think about and pray for while reading the book.

2. PRAY – Ask God to do something big in your life as you continue to read this book. Ask Him to open your eyes to your place in the kingdom and open your eyes to people He wants you to minister to.

Seed Life Spotlight
CATHERINE'S STORY
By Sherrill Auker

The loud and impassioned prayers of 200 Zambian leaders echoed against the pavilion's metal roof. They were divided according to their 19 chiefdoms, each group believing for the Kingdom of heaven to come in their own communities. Standing, as the watchmen Isaiah 62 describes, "all the day and all the night they shall never be silent."[22] Men and women of God reminding the Lord of His promises, not allowing Him to rest until His words are established in their sight.

Few are Bible school graduates or formally trained ministers. Instead, they are farmers and small-business owners, average community members who decided to take God at His Word. They've read the teachings of Jesus and simply demonstrated belief. He said, "Go and make disciples," so they host revival meetings.[23] "Whoever believes in me will also do the works that I do," so they see the sick healed.[24] "Ask and it will be given to you," and His provision is before them.[25]

Catherine is among the attendees. A middle-aged woman, strong from a life of farm labor and raising five children. She stands out now as a leader among the group, the Word always on her tongue, her heart open to the Lord. We met six years ago at the most challenging training we had done to date.

For the last eight years, I have been a missionary with Overland Missions, an interdenominational Christian ministry based in Florida and internationally headquartered near Livingstone, Zambia. Our agricultural branch, Sustain, provides educational opportunities for rural farmers, focusing on the discipleship program Farming God's Way (FGW). Mimicking the principles God has displayed in His own garden, the natural landscape, we can improve soil health, increase yields, and tangibly see God's provision. Operating on a strict "no hand-outs" policy, we teach communities to use what is already in their hands.

We sat in Chili Village of the Nyawa Chiefdom, waiting for interested community members. Late starting events were not unusual in the laidback culture, but this three hour delay was a stretch. With four people, we began teaching, allowing others to trickle in upon arrival. Though my introductory session was met with apathy, Gertrude, my teammate, continued on, addressing issues of witchcraft, the tendency to trust other things rather than God. The atmosphere shifted as attendees, surprised by the Scriptures Gertrude was reading, sparked an interactive Bible study.

We stayed at Catherine's home that night, and her family hosted our demonstration the following morning. She made her first FGW planting rope, not yet realizing its potential impact.

Using local resources, Catherine put her learning into practice. Within the first season, the positive changes were evident. Her garden became a billboard of God's goodness and she, the vocal messenger who couldn't remain quiet.

Catherine's walk with the Lord continued to grow and develop. When He healed her body of a strange semi-paralysis, her faith deepened, and her testimony spread. As a volunteer orphan caregiver, Catherine was responsible for monitoring the state of orphans in her community, ensuring they were well cared for by extended family. During her third FGW season, government officers with the caregiver program stopped by her home. Overjoyed by her garden results, Catherine drug the officers down the mile-long path to the site. They were astounded, "You have to teach the other 90+ caregivers!"

Gertrude and I drove the rough rocky roads a few days later. Catherine relayed the events, obviously nervous at the suggestions of the government officials, balking at the opportunity presented. Catherine hadn't gone to school and didn't know English. She questioned her ability to pass on Farming God's Way to others . Gertrude, at this point three years a trainer, spoke up, "You know I never finished school, right?" Gertrude, a powerful minister of the gospel, was unable to fund her own schooling past ninth grade. Upon hearing this news, Catherine's own faith was built up. She followed up with the officers and started to teach FGW trainings. When one person chooses to believe the Word and walk in the power of the Holy Spirit, it frees others to do the same. Even now, Catherine is thriving, with new members joining her all the time.

Our training team walks fields with Catherine, visiting new participants that she has recruited. Matildah's home marked the end of one long venture on dirt paths and across dry riverbeds.

Catherine's FGW group ministered to her, a widow of three years, a victim of property-grabbing. After her husband's death, his parents and siblings took everything, leaving two children with no possible income generation. Farm equipment and tools vanished along with hope for their future. But Catherine saw promise. Matildah met us with bowls of tomatoes, armloads of maize cobs, and overflowing gratitude. When all seemed lost, her neighboring missionary-farmers arrived at the homestead. From Gertrude to Catherine to Matildah: a ripple effect of unschooled, ordinary people's ministry.

> *Now when they saw the boldness of Peter and John, and perceived that they were uneducated, common men, they were astonished. And they recognized that they had been with Jesus.[26]*

In 1 Corinthians 1:26-27, Paul urges the church of Corinth to consider their calling. How many were wise according to the world? Or powerful? Or of noble birth? Rather, God chooses the humble, the seemingly foolish, the weak. Christ Jesus himself is our wisdom, righteousness, sanctification, and redemption. When we understand "Christ in us," we can live in His confidence, for His glory.

While the early church continued to multiply, a complaint arose: a group of widows were being neglected in the daily distribution of food. The disciples were brought together, and an announcement was made, "It is not right that we should give up preaching the word of God to serve tables."[27] An election of seven men was proposed as a solution, men of "good repute, full of the Spirit and of wisdom" appointed to the care of the vulnerable.

Stephen was among them. His story is captured in two brief chapters of Acts. This man, chosen to manage food aid, did not settle in to today's definition of layman, rather "full of grace and power, was doing great wonders and signs among the people."[28] Filled with the Holy Spirit, the natural outflow of his life was so powerful, he was deemed a danger to the status quo.

Stephen, confronted by the high priest, delivered a bold message in direct opposition of the religious leaders. Before they threw the first stone, he saw Jesus standing with the Father. The heavens opened to him and revealed God's glory. At this declaration, the crowd rushed him, threw him out of the city, and ended his life. He, like the One who went before, made two requests of the Father in his last moments. With forgiveness for his enemies, Stephen asked the Lord to receive his spirit and fell asleep.

We can categorize Stephen as a powerful apostle, differentiating us, the average church-goer, from his passionate life. But in reality, today, we would simply label his role as layman or deacon. He would have the opportunity to function as a humanitarian, task-focused and people-centered. The apostles, pastors, and missionaries are those with bold messages, while the rest of the church serves with their hands and not their mouths.

2 Corinthians 5 offers a more accurate perspective:

Therefore if anyone is in Christ, he is a new creation. The old has passed away; behold, the new has come. All this is from God, who through Christ reconciled us to himself and gave us the ministry of reconciliation; that is, in Christ God was reconciling the world to himself, not counting their trespasses against them, and entrusting to us the message of reconciliation.[29]

"Minister" is not a title for a select few, but rather the title of every person who accepts the new life Christ offers. We have placed limitations on ourselves while exalting others, attempting to lessen our role. But the biblical expectation is that every Jesus follower would walk as a minister of reconciliation. We were chosen as carriers of the same message we've experienced, ambassadors of our original family. Stephen understood his true responsibility as a "layman." Do we?

Our daily decisions and priorities are a reflection of how well we grasp our identity in Christ. Romans 6 says, "...just as Christ was raised from the dead by the glory of the Father, we too might walk in newness of life."[30] Paul then urges us to "consider yourselves dead to sin and alive to God in Christ Jesus."[31] The work is finished, leaving us only to believe it to be so. If we take on this mantel, living "alive to God," His Word will naturally pour from us. Our hearts will beat for the nations, and our desire will be first and foremost for the advancement of His kingdom. We have everything in us to be the Stephen, the Catherine of our community, rising up with a passion for His glory and ministering His reconciliation with freedom and power.

2
Soil-Building
PREPARATION FOR THE SEED

As my wife, my son, and I stood over the unopened box in our basement I remember saying to myself, "I think we are officially crossing a line." For Christmas two years earlier, my sister-in-law had given us most of the things we needed to make an indoor vermicomposting system. Now, if you don't know what "vermicomposting" is, it is the process of using worms to digest food scraps and turn them into soil. In laymen's terms, you basically put worms into a box, set up the right environment, throw in food scraps and other elements, and after a few months you are left with rich, healthy soil. Vermicompost is some of the most fertile and nutrient rich soil you can find.

Still, as I looked at the package lying there on our washing machine knowing it was full of thousands of worms, I felt like we were crossing a line into hippy weirdness. I mean, we had been gardening and trying to grow our own food for several years, but who in the world decides to let worms live in their house? People have dogs and cats, not a colony of worms.

After wrestling with these questions and feelings, I finally decided to just open the box. My son, who was three at the time anxiously awaited the unveiling. I cut into the box, opened up the bag inside and poured out the worms. There before me was this writhing, slimy mass that looked disgusting. I was both intrigued and grossed out. My son on the other hand was pumped to get in there. He reached down and started to pick up the worms by the handful and move them around. He and I worked on getting their house ready for a while and soon everything was set. All that was left to do was to put food scraps into the system, keep everything moist, and the worms would do the rest.

Now, you might ask why I am telling you this story. For one, I wanted someone else to relive the trauma of that moment with me. But the real reason I bring it up is due to why we decided to have worms in the first place. You see, vermicompost is some of the best compost you could ever add into your soil in a garden. And as I learned more about gardening over the years, I started to realize the truth of these axioms, "A garden is only as good as its soil" and "if you want to feed plants you have to feed the soil."

These kinds of statements are often used in a style of gardening I have studied called permaculture. Permaculture is a way of thinking about gardening in terms of replicating and enhancing nature instead of trying to fight it. I learned some of the concepts I now utilize through Paul Gautschi. He is a gardener who lives in Washington state and is featured in a documentary called "Back to Eden."[32] In this documentary, he recalls being frustrated as he looked at his garden because it was struggling despite his constant effort.

He says he talked to God about this frustration one day and God told him to look toward the forest near his property. The trees were green and full of life. He asked why this was and God pointed him to the soil and the natural way that soil was built up. Every year, the trees dropped their leaves and covered the soil. Soil life, like worms, came in to process the material that had fallen. It was left undisturbed except for the normal, natural disturbance of weather and animals.

Based on what he observed, instead of tilling his soil, he started to simply cover his soil with rich compost and wood chips. Not only did it require far less work from him over time, but he started to see his garden become more and more productive. The axioms held true in his case. As Paul Gautschi fed his soil, it fed his plants. And instead of tilling his soil like everyone else, he decided to simply build soil by covering it with compost and mulch. We decided to practice some of these same principles in our garden. In order to build the best possible soil we were willing to do anything, even raising worms in our basement.

Not only have our gardens been more productive since we started doing this, but I feel like God has used it to give me some spiritual insights as well. Before we start talking about sowing the seeds of the Kingdom in other peoples' lives, we first need to consider the soil. Probably Jesus' most famous parable about soil is the parable of the sower. In Mark 4:3-8 it says:

> *Listen! A farmer went out to sow his seed. As he was scattering the seed, some fell along the path, and the birds came and ate it up. Some fell on rocky places, where it did not have much soil. It sprang up*

quickly, because the soil was shallow. But when the sun came up, the plants were scorched, and they withered because they had no root. Other seed fell among thorns, which grew up and choked the plants, so that they did not bear grain. Still other seed fell on good soil. It came up, grew and produced a crop, some multiplying thirty, some sixty, some a hundred times.[33]

As is usually the case, the disciples are a little confused about Jesus' parable. Later on in Mark 4:14-20, Jesus explains the parable to them:

The farmer sows the word. Some people are like seed along the path where the word is sown. As soon as they hear it, Satan comes and takes away the word that was sown in them. Others, like seed sown on rocky places, hear the word and at once receive it with joy. But since they have no root, they last only a short time. When trouble or persecution comes because of the word, they quickly fall away. Still others, like seed sown among thorns, hear the word; but the worries of this life, the deceitfulness of wealth and the desires for other things come in and choke the word, making it unfruitful. Others, like seed sown on good soil, hear the word, accept it, and produce a crop – some thirty, some sixty, some a hundred times what was sown.[34]

The seed in the parable is the Word of God, the Truth. It is the only thing that has the power to transform the heart of the person receiving it. However, in the parable the emphasis is not on the Word itself because the Word of God and the Truth of who He is always remains the same. The point of the parable is the receptivity of the hearts of the people.

Donald English puts it this way: "The central clue in the parable is found in the various types of receptivity in the ground. Neither the sower nor the seed (and certainly not the weather!) are determinative. Everything depends on the state of the ground."[35] He also adds this:

> *If C.H. Dodd was right in claiming that the meaning of a parable will be a 'kingdom' meaning, that is, a truth related to the kingdom of God, then the parable of the sower is explaining why some respond and enter, while others do not, when the grace of God is freely available to all.*[36]

Have you ever wondered why it seems like some of the people you reach out to with the message of the Gospel and church and faith are willing to hear you out and others are not? Have you ever wondered why you can ask two very similar people to join a Bible study or come to church and one will say yes while the other says no? The reason is the state of the soil of their heart.

In my book, *Engage: How to Know God*, I made the case that before we ever get to the point of surrendering our lives to God and accepting the message of the Gospel, two other things must happen. First, we must be humbled by God's eternal Truth, meaning we must come to terms with the fact that there is a God and we are not Him. Second, we must be broken to have a new heart, meaning we must recognize that we are not good people who have occasionally done some bad things, but we are "dead-hearted" people who need to receive a brand new heart from God.

The point I make in *Engage: How to Know God* is if we cannot acknowledge these two things as true, then why would we ever accept the message of the Gospel? Our hearts would not be prepared to receive the Truth, because if we are ever going to accept the Gospel as true, we obviously must first accept that there is a God. And to accept the need for salvation by what Jesus did through His death and resurrection, we must also accept that we are people who need saving.

If someone is not convinced in their heart of the need to be humbled by God's eternal Truth and be broken to have a new heart, then we can sow all the seed we want in their life, but it will never grow. The soil of their heart is not ready. The dilemma is, how do we participate with God in preparing the soil of their heart?

TILLING THE SOIL

I believe part of the reason we find this process so difficult to do in the lives of people around us is because we are convinced there is only one way to prepare the hearts of people around us: by tilling. The dictionary defines the word "till" this way: "to labor, as by plowing or harrowing, upon (land) for the raising of crops; cultivate."[37] Almost all farmers and gardeners use this as their primary means of preparing the soil to receive seed. The theory behind it is that the hard, weedy ground needs to be broken up in order to be loose enough to support the roots of growing plants.

Tilling is a very labor-intensive process. Farmers need to use large, heavy, expensive equipment to plow their large fields. Home gardeners either need to have a rototiller or need to use some sort of hand implement to strike the ground and loosen it up. As you break into the hard ground, you discover rocks and roots of trees and weeds and various other things that would not allow plants to grow well in the soil. The process of tilling hard soil just seems to make sense. It is even utilized as a picture in Scripture. In Hosea 10:12-13a it says:

Sow righteousness for yourselves, reap the fruit of unfailing love, and break up your unplowed ground; for it is time to seek the Lord, until he comes and showers his righteousness on you. But you have planted wickedness, you have reaped evil, you have eaten the fruit of deception.[38]

In the passage, God is speaking to Israel and showing them the self-reliance they have been living with. Instead of depending on Him, they have been depending on their own might. He encourages them to "break up your unplowed ground."[39] In this case, a battle was going to come against them and they would be devastated, but you can see in God's encouragement that He wishes their hearts would not be so hard as to need this level of discipline to get their attention.

Tilling is an intensive process, often violent, and it takes physical strength or strong equipment to accomplish it. In a similar way, when we consider that "tilling" the hearts of people around us is the only way to prepare the soil of their hearts to receive the Word of God, we will have some very clear expectations.

First, the tone of that preparation process will be confrontational. You do not come out and dance and sing over your soil to till it. You do not read poetry to your soil to till it. You do not lovingly hug the soil or encourage the soil to till it. You exert powerful and aggressive forces on the soil to loosen it up.

Do you have a similar picture toward preparing the hearts of people around you to hear the Gospel? When someone finds out you are a Christian and they start mocking you, how do you respond? When someone comes at you with facts and figures in their attempt to prove God and faith are phony, how do you respond? When your family member whom you love

43

dearly continually resists any kind of conversations toward faith, how do you respond?

Do you think in your mind, "I am not ready for this. I have to become more mentally prepared to take this on because this is going to be a battle." Do you think, "How am I going to defend God in this situation?" Or "I do not like how they are talking about my faith. I have to make sure they know they are wrong."

If this is your natural response, it is understandable. We desperately want the people around us to know Jesus. In the physical realm and in most conversations of the day, the need to respond with swift action would seem to be the most sensible course. Do not get me wrong. There will be times we may be called by God to lovingly but boldly speak the Truth or let someone suffer just consequences in order for their heart to be plowed and prepared for the Word of God.

My concern, though, is if we think of tilling the hearts of people around us as the only or even primary means of preparing the soil of their hearts, then we will have so many excuses come up as to why we cannot evangelize people around us. When we think of the strength and intensity necessary to till the soil of someone else's heart, here are some of the excuses we might come up with:

"I am not strong enough to reach out like that because they might reject me and I am not sure whether I can handle that."

"I do not know enough to confront my friend or family member. They are way smarter than me and I do not know enough about God and the Bible yet."

"I am not good with confrontation, so I will just let other people who are good at confrontation do evangelism."

"I do not have the tools I need to do this. I need to make sure I do it perfectly or they may not go to heaven."

"What if I get something wrong? I would never forgive myself."

Do you hear the message behind all of these? In the end, they all come back to *"me."* I am not strong enough, smart enough, confrontational enough, equipped enough, and perfect enough to do this correctly. Just as a gardener cannot imagine a fertile, healthy soil without their active tilling, so we cannot imagine this sort of evangelism without our intervention. And it always leaves us feeling short of where we need to be.

I have talked to many people recently about evangelism. The particular group that interested me most were those who have been Christians for a really long time, even decades. What I observed is in general, the newer the believer, the more likely they were to reach out to other people. There are several reasons why this would make sense. For instance, a new believer probably has many more close connections to people who are not in the faith. Also, the initial transformation of someone who has started a relationship with God is often so dramatic that people cannot help but notice.

Despite all of those reasons, the reality is we should grow more and more passionate about sharing the Gospel, not less. I started gardening around five years ago. Would it make sense for me to have the same size garden or a smaller garden now than I did five years ago if I really was passionate about growing food? Not at all. If I was really passionate about it then I would constantly be thinking about how to expand my ability and area to be able to grow more and more food. I am growing probably twenty-five times the amount of food now that I was growing back then. It is just the normal progression of things.

So why is it that people who have been Christians for decades are far less active at sharing the Gospel than they were back at the start of their faith journey? Surprisingly, the comments I've heard most refer to an unpreparedness to evangelize people. They had a lack of confidence in their knowledge of faith. What if someone brought up a question that they did not know how to answer? They did not want to make a splash and confront people directly. What if that person was driven further from Jesus instead of closer? Fear and hesitancy immobilize so many from the wonderful Kingdom purpose they have been given.

The irony is that many folks who have these fears have been in Bible study after Bible study and heard sermon after sermon. Most of them have read and understood a majority of the Bible. How in the world can they feel like they aren't knowledgeable enough? Simply because they do not know as much as their pastor, who received a bachelor's degree or master's degree in theology? Perhaps because they do not know as much as that one man or woman in their Bible study? What is going on here?

I think the reason for this hesitancy is multifaceted. However, the primary reason can become systemic in most of our churches. Whether we realize it or not, the way we approach church can over time encourage people to depend on themselves. In my position as Pastor of Spiritual Formation at our church I am keenly aware of this. If we are not careful, we can give the impression that the only way to grow in your faith is to achieve increasingly new levels of intellectual knowledge. Now, intellectual knowledge is essential to growing with God, but it is not the *only* thing necessary. 2 Peter 3:18 says, "But grow in the grace and knowledge of our Lord and Savior Jesus Christ."[40] We do not need merely intellectual knowledge, but also experiential knowledge of the grace of God to keep growing in our faith.

When our intellectual knowledge of God keeps growing but our experience of God does not, an internal struggle begins within us. Without even realizing it, we start to feel like a hypocrite. We know so much, but we cannot even live up to what we know. We start to look inward more than outward, trying to fix the disparity. We run from class to small group to church sermons to sermon podcasts to counseling in an attempt to fix ourselves. I am not saying that any of these things are wrong, but if we keep going to these places without actually practicing what we learn, we will start to become more and more confused and more content to depend on our own strength instead of God's. We will start to think the amount of knowledge we have of God is what proves our devotion instead of the actual practice of that knowledge. As the Apostle Paul says in 1 Corinthians 8:1, "But knowledge puffs up while love builds up."[41]

What does this have to do with evangelism? Well, two things can happen when we keep growing in our intellectual knowledge of God but not our experience of God. Either we can become really aggressive and destructive in our evangelism toward others or more often what happens is we can become terrified of sharing our faith. We become terrified because we increasingly put more of the pressure to evangelize on ourselves and our own knowledge instead of God.

Some people use this vast amount of knowledge to come at people with pointed Bible verses, seeking to till as violently as possible into their heart because they take their job of evangelism very seriously. Many times these conversations and relationships can become very aggressive and toxic. The people they are reaching out to start to feel like projects instead of people. They feel the need to be defensive because the tone of the conversations is always attacking.

Unfortunately, even if the Christian speaks Truth in this situation, their life does not demonstrate the truth of what they are saying. This breaks my heart, because without knowing it, these well-meaning Christians have done far more damage to the cause of Christ in that person's life than if they had done nothing at all. A person usually comes away from these types of relationships saying, "If that is what a Christian looks like, then I want nothing to do with it."

Most people, though, simply take on more and more of the responsibility of tilling the soil in other peoples' lives and it incapacitates them. They never feel prepared enough, godly enough, good enough, etc. Well, the truth is we are *never* prepared enough, godly enough, or good enough at evangelism to prepare the soil of someone's heart. But God is. In fact, He is the *only* one who can work the soil of the heart to prepare it for the seed of life to take root. We are simply His co-workers in the process.

That is why I believe that tilling to prepare the hearts of others is not the best picture of what we are meant to do. God has been teaching me a new picture of what He wants as I work the soil in my own back yard.

A DIFFERENT WAY

Did you know there are trillions of organisms in your backyard doing very specific tasks in the soil? Joel Salatin says, "Actually, soil – I refuse to call it dirt because that has such degrading connotations – is a pulsing, thriving community of beings. One cupped handful contains more beings than there are people on the face of the earth."[42] Can you believe that? One little handful of soil contains more beings than there are people on our entire planet.

Not only are those organisms there but they have very specific jobs to do in the soil. Below our feet, there is a dance going on with some beings breaking down nutrients, others transforming them, while others transport them. They all work together in harmony to bring about healthy plants and vegetables we can eat.

The more I understand about creation, the more insane it seems to believe that all of this came here by accident. There is a unity and harmony to how things act in nature. Each being is a part of a puzzle, transferring the sun's rays, water, and nutrients into plants and vegetables. Incredible! Now, there are some destructive beings in the soil as well, just as there are always good bacteria and harmful bacteria doing battle within our bodies on a daily basis.

The point is, just as our bodies are finely tuned machines, what if the soil is a finely tuned machine as well? What if God has already put inside the soil the means by which it can become fertile and productive? What if all we need to do is to make the right environment and the soil will most likely do what it was designed to do?

This is the type of gardening I have been practicing for a few years. Basically, I cover patches of weeds and hard soil with newspaper, paper, or cardboard. On top of that I put a thick layer of compost. If you have been wondering what compost is as I have used the word, it is "a mixture of various decaying organic substances, as dead leaves or manure, used for fertilizing soil."[43] You can use all kinds of things to make compost: kitchen scraps, grass clippings, leaves, manure, paper, cardboard, etc. God has designed composting as a way to take green elements in nature and brown elements in nature, mix them together, and have the end result be very loose and fertile soil.

After I put the newspaper/cardboard/paper and the compost down, I put a layer of decomposing wood chips on top to mulch the soil. I do not do any major tilling; I simply cover the soil. It is incredible to watch what happens. Where before there was hard, weedy soil, this incredibly rich, loose soil emerges over time. The compost and mulch retain moisture and smother the weeds. The loose nature of the soil allows for the roots of plants to travel deep and start to break up the soil. Most importantly, it provides the right atmosphere for good soil life.

Believe it or not, when you till the soil it kills off many of the organisms that would be helpful in developing rich, healthy soil. When you do not till the soil, but instead provide the right atmosphere for them by building the soil up, the soil organisms, insects, and worms all begin to till the soil for you. After a year or so of this process, the soil underneath is completely unrecognizable from what it was before, but I had little to do with it. I just made the right conditions by building the soil up.

So what has God been teaching me about evangelism through this? What if preparation of the hearts of people around us is so much more about soil-*building* than soil-*tilling*?

What if it is so much more about God's work in this process than ours? What if God has already put the elements in place to prepare the hearts of people and our only job is to encourage a right atmosphere and environment?

In Ecclesiastes 3:11 it says, "He has also set eternity in the human heart…"[44] This verse has always struck me. There is something deep within us that knows there is something bigger than us. Despite how much we may try to run from the feeling, despite how much we may try to cover it up, despite how sinful we are, there is something within us that is drawn toward the truth of eternity. In the same way those organisms within the soil are prepared to do the work if given the right environment, there is an underlying inkling deep within us that there is something out there bigger than us. There is a hole in our hearts that is not satisfied with earthly pleasures.

Before you think I am saying our salvation comes from within us, the Bible teaches that before we know God, we are dead in our trespasses and sins. We are incapable of taking any steps toward God. In fact, John 6:44 says, "No one can come to me unless the Father who sent me draws them."[45] And John 6:65 says, "This is why I told you that no one can come to me unless the Father has enabled them."[46] Only God can make a dead heart prepared enough to receive the Truth of the Gospel.

This is where the theology term, *prevenient grace*, comes in. Prevenient grace means that by God's grace, He not only saves us, but He does the work to draw us toward salvation in the first place. So how do we participate with Him in this?

We don't have the power to draw people, loosen up that soil of their heart, or prepare the way for the seed of the Gospel. This is important for us to realize. It is not the awesome band, the amazing preacher, the succinct evangelistic message, or the humorous Christian video that will prepare the soil of the human heart. God alone can accomplish this. Everything we do simply prepares the environment or hinders the environment for God to do His work.

HOW DOES THIS LOOK?

If our primary role in preparing the soil of people's hearts is to be soil-builders, then how does it look? This could be played out in many different ways, but I believe there are three primary categories of ways we can build soil in the lives of the people around us.

SACRIFICIAL LOVE

In the world of gardening there is a term called "chop and drop." It sounds very violent and mysterious, but it is actually something very simple. In order to keep soil loose and fertile, the concept is you simply prune off part of a plant and drop the material from the plant on the soil below it. This process helps the plant in several ways.

First, by covering the soil, you are helping it resist drying out or hardening when it does not rain. Second, as the plant material breaks down it feeds the soil, making it more fertile. Third, you are providing an atmosphere where worms and other creatures want to live. As they break down the plant material, they gently till the soil and loosen it up.

As I thought about building soil, the first picture that came to mind was: if God is the one doing the work and we are simply working together with Him to prepare the right environment in the hearts of people around us, I cannot think of a better way than sacrificial love. And I cannot think of a better picture of sacrificial love than doing a "chop and drop" on a plant.

Remember how I said that in our picture of the Kingdom of God as a garden, Jesus was the seed of life planted in the soil? Through His death and resurrection, that Gospel message or seed of life multiplied and was available to anyone. When we surrender our lives to God's grace through Jesus it is as though that seed of life is planted in the good soil of our hearts.

If we grow in our faith, as is expected through the work of God in us, then we grow into strong and healthy plants that start to produce fruit (i.e. the fruit of the Sprit: love, joy, peace, patience, kindness, goodness, faithfulness, and self-control). When that fruit is full grown and falls off into the soil around us, we continue to seed the Gospel message into receptive soil (or the receptive hearts of people) around us. However, we can be producing fruit in our lives and still not find people around us receptive to the message of the Gospel. This is the whole reason why the first step in sharing the Gospel with other people is participating with God in soil-building.

Consider this picture with me. We said earlier that if we consider tilling the soil to be our job, we will be confrontational and aggressive in our evangelism. Often, this only hardens the soil of the hearts of people around us. But what if God wants to do something incredible, something only God would think of? What if in the Kingdom of God, God wants to prune us to keep us growing, while also using that pruning to prepare the hearts of others?

The Bible is clear that God prunes us to make us more fruitful. In John 15:1-2 it says, "I am the true vine, and my father is the gardener. He cuts off every branch in me that bears no fruit, while every branch that does bear fruit he prunes so that it will be even more fruitful."[47] God already promises to prune our lives to make us more fruitful, but what if that pruning is also meant to prepare the hearts of others? What if God wants to free us to sacrifice our time, money, and energy to prepare the hearts of others?

I have been to many conferences, retreats, and Christian concerts. A common occurrence at these events is to have someone from an organization like Compassion International or World Vision come and talk about supporting a child in another country. Most of the people in the audience came into that event without thinking there was much room in their budgets for flexibility. As the presenter runs through how only $30 a month can change the life of someone around the world, you see people start to consider how they could be part of showing love to someone they've never met. The kicker is when the presenter talks about the average amount we spend on something like coffee during a month that is obviously far less important than another person's life.

In that moment, for some people God is talking to, there is a pruning going on. All of a sudden, there is a realization of how a small financial sacrifice on their part could show love to someone the whole way across the world. I have been this person on at least one occasion. And whether I realized it or not, in that moment I was participating with God in soil-building. God was pruning something out of me financially that He was going to use to cover the soil of someone else's heart. In that moment I was participating in the Kingdom of God.

The amazing part is how things multiply in the Kingdom of God, just like in nature. In my garden, when I do a "chop and drop" on a plant, what I find is the plant becomes healthier and the soil around it becomes healthier as well. In that moment of supporting a child, God confronted wastefulness in my own heart, while using my step of obedient sacrifice to prepare the soil in someone else's heart.

This is one simple example, but it still might feel far off. Let's make it a little more personal. What about the spouse who does not know Jesus yet? I have talked to many Christian spouses that get so frustrated because of the unbelief of their significant others. I have sat with many tearful men and women who yearn for their spouse to come into a saving relationship with Jesus.

Many times, as I listen, there is a tension in them. Sometimes it is hard to not let frustration and anger come into their marriage. Sometimes it comes in the form of marital conflict caused by their spouse not being on the same page spiritually. Other times they so badly want their spouse to know Jesus that they are forceful in sharing the Gospel with them and it causes frustration and anger on both sides. They are at a loss for what to do.

One passage I usually take them to is 1 Peter 3:1-2. In this passage, Peter is speaking specifically to wives, but the principle could be applied to men or women. Peter says, "Wives, in the same way submit yourselves to your own husbands so that, if any of them do not believe the word, they may be won over without words by the behavior of their wives, when they see the purity and reverence of your lives."[48]

Despite the frustrations and anger and fighting that occur in a marriage with an unbelieving spouse, not to mention the inherent dissatisfaction that comes with living with someone who has a different worldview, Peter does not counsel spouses to be more forceful in sharing the Gospel. He applies the principles of soil-building. His basic message is to let God continue to prune away your own desires and dreams. Give sacrificially, even if the other person does not deserve it, and through your love the soil of their hearts will be prepared to hear the Gospel.

I have watched people live out this passage. I specifically remember several wives who had unbelieving husbands truly taking this passage to heart. They would be put in difficult situations; their husband would taunt them about faith and try to keep them from giving too much of their time, money, and energy to the work of God. Many times, those wives yearned for husbands who would help lead the family spiritually.

But instead of giving into anger, fear, and anxiety about their situation, these wives turned their attention to God. God pruned away their bitterness, frustration, and dissatisfaction and they lived lives of peace with their husbands. When their husband finally did come to Jesus, it was primarily because the sacrificial love of his wife led him to think that this "Jesus-thing" must be true.

There are so many other ways this could apply:

NEIGHBORS – Do you ignore opportunities with your neighbors because of neighborhood drama or lack of time? Maybe God wants to prune out your pride or lead you to sacrifice some of your "me-time" to give to your neighbors.

CHILDREN – Are you willing to spend significant amounts of time and energy on work or a hobby, while not investing that same kind of energy into your kids? Maybe God wants to prune out that idol and lead you to give the same type of time and energy to your kids.

CO-WORKERS – Do you want to make a difference in the lives of your unbelieving coworkers, but you feel like a hypocrite because you are doing and saying the same ungodly things they do and say? Maybe God wants to prune those sin issues out of your life, and give you a clear conscience to be able to show your coworkers a different way.

Sacrificial love is one of the most powerful ways we can be soil-builders. In the end, we are simply emulating the life of Jesus. In Philippians 2:5-8 it says:

In your relationship with one another, have the same mindset as Christ Jesus: Who, being in the very nature God, did not consider equality with God something to be used to his own advantage; rather, he made himself nothing by taking the very nature of a servant, being made in human likeness. And being found in appearance as a man, he humbled himself by becoming obedient to death – even death on a cross.[49]

HEARTFELT QUESTIONS

Another way to be a soil-builder is to use heartfelt questions. When you actually read through what Jesus says in the Gospels it is interesting how often He does not directly answer someone's question. Most often He answers questions with questions.

The famous Christian apologist Ravi Zacharias often points this out in his teaching and gives several reasons for why he believes Jesus uses questions this way. One reason is to judge the right starting point for the conversation. Sometimes what people are asking is not really what needs answering.

Tom Price, writing under the banner of Ravi Zacharias' ministry, also says this about questions, "Questions can help us to concentrate, pay attention, and think together. A good question can transform a meandering discussion into a life-changing moment, when reality breaks through illusion."[50]

I have found that more often than not, my job with an unbeliever is not to try to convince them of the truth of Jesus but to ask them questions that help them think through their own worldview. Every single one of us acts, thinks, and feels the way we do because of what we believe. Yet, the reality is most people do not think about what they actually believe on a daily basis. This is why I believe questions, if asked in a heartfelt and loving way, are one of the most powerful tools in regard to preparing the soil of another person's heart.

It reminds me of dandelions. Dandelions are the sworn enemy of landscapers and many homeowners. But even weeds have a purpose in nature. Dandelions are edible; the leaves and flowers can be eaten raw or cooked. The root can actually be used to make a tea that is like a coffee substitute. Beyond that, dandelions are useful in nature in that they most often grow in compacted or hard soil and have a deep tap root compared to most other weeds. This root grows and pushes down into the soil to loosen it up and prepare it to be more fertile.

Imagine your questions are like dandelion seeds you are planting in the lives of your family and friends. Our hope is that these questions we ask would be sown into the hard soil of their heart and God might use our questions to open up space for them to hear the Truth of the Gospel.

The best questions delve into areas of a person's worldview or beliefs about their existence. Ravi Zacharias breaks down the key elements of someone's worldview as origin (where do we come from), meaning (why do we exist), morality (how should we live), and destiny (where are we going).[51] Here are some examples of scenarios where these questions might come up:

NATURE-LOVING FRIEND – You have a friend who loves to be out in nature and take walks. Because you like spending time with them, you decide to go on a hike with them nearby. Now, that hike could simply be a hike or it could be an opportunity for soil-building. During the walk, as you look at the majesty of nature, it would be easy to start talking about the beauty around you. A simple, but powerful question might be, "Have you ever thought about where this all came from?" Can you imagine the interesting places this conversation could go? In the process, you could share your belief about God creating it all.

NEGATIVE CO-WORKER – You have a friend who comes in every day looking gloomy and depressed. No matter what happens in the office, they can never see the positive side. They have noticed you have a sense of hope and joy despite tough work conditions and ask how you always remain so positive. In the midst of the conversation, you could ask them a question of meaning like, "So what do you think this life is all about" or "why do you think we exist?" This could open great doors to talk about the hope of the Gospel.

NONCHALANT FAMILY MEMBER – You have a family member who is going through life casually, doing whatever they want and not really caring about the consequences. Asking them questions like, "How do you determine what is right for you to do" or "do you believe in right and wrong" or "do you think there will be any lasting consequences beyond this life for your decisions" might start a conversation about morality or destiny.

There are many other questions you could ask. If you ask questions with sincerity and are honestly looking for an answer, the good thing is most people will not be offended to talk about them. And when you think they've gotten to a point where you could share part of your story or the Gospel with them, you will know exactly what to talk to them about. This is why when I meet with someone seeking counsel, I usually spend at least the first fifteen to thirty minutes asking them questions. Only then can I actually answer the question they really have on their heart.

PRAYER

Sacrificial love and heartfelt questions are great tools for soil-building, but the most important tool is prayer. Remember, it is ultimately God who loosens up the soil of someone's heart and draws that person to a relationship with Him. Because this is the case, prayer is an essential element to soil-building.

Oswald J. Smith in his book *The Work God Blesses* says, "The highest form of Christian service is intercessory prayer."[52] In fact, later in the book he says: The greatest thing that the apostles could possibly do for the Kingdom of God was to give themselves first to prayer, then to the ministry of the Word. And you will notice that prayer precedes preaching."[53] In this quote, he is referencing Acts 6:4, where the apostles in the early church commit themselves to focusing their energy on nothing else except prayer and the Word. Smith's point is that they gave themselves first to prayer and then to sharing the Gospel with people.

I have often wondered what would be different if we were to spend as much time praying for people and our communities as we did trying to do things to reach them. I must say this has been a significant struggle for me in the past. I have always believed in the power of prayer, but in the past it was easier for me to study the Bible and think deeply about things instead of depending on God through prayer. When I would read something in Scripture or think about something interesting I would often just try to reach out to people in my own strength instead of preparing the way through prayer.

Thankfully, I have been surrounded by a great group of pastors and leaders at our church who have both demonstrated and encouraged me to always go to God in prayer first. Our church staff spends significant time in prayer together beyond just our own personal prayer lives. We have a daily gathering for prayer in the morning. We meet as a staff once a month to devote part of a work day to prayer. We pray before almost every meeting we have, but this is not just rote prayer; you can tell the people who are praying truly mean what they say.

The message is always the same: "God, if you do not do the work in _____ (this meeting, this person's life, my heart, this situation) we have no power to change it. But we believe You have the power and ask You to make a way for Your power to be released in this situation." Being around a team like this and watching their lives has helped me keep in mind the need I have to pray continually for the people in my life who do not know Jesus yet.

Praying for someone to be open to the gospel is like praying for rain. A key ingredient to building soil in a garden is water. If you do not have water over an extended period of time it hinders the ability of mulch and compost to break down. Now, you can try to water the soil with a hose, but that only lasts for a while. The greatest thing you could receive is a long-soaking rain. But obviously, we do not control the rain. We have no power over when it comes and goes. But God does.

In the same way we can pray for rain to come over our farm or garden, we need to pray for the rain of God's grace to prepare the soil of the hearts of the people around us. His grace will allow those heartfelt questions and sacrificial love to build soil in the hearts of people and prepare them for the seed of life to be sown in them.

CONCLUSION

I was watching an online video recently of a traveling pastor and evangelist named Todd White. I am not sure if I would exactly agree with everything Todd believes theologically; I do not know enough about him. But there was a testimony he told that I think demonstrates this picture of soil-building well.

Todd tells the story of how God led him to a local Guitar Center. Inside, he met a guy named Jesse who was playing one of the store's guitars. Unbeknownst to Todd, he was there almost every day. Through a series of loving conversations, heartfelt questions, and prayer Jesse started to open up about what was going on in his heart. His dad had committed suicide ten years earlier. He had pain from this and was also struggling through a drug addiction.

Todd felt as though God was asking him to pray over Jesse for physical healing and when he did, Jesse felt something happen inside of him. It freaked him out, but Todd explained that God was able to do anything, even heal him of something physically. Jesse was so excited about this that he called his girlfriend, mom, and daughter who were next door shopping, wanting them to meet Todd. Todd prayed for them too. Then, without being weird about it or having strings attached, Todd felt led to pay for the clothes they were buying. As he was paying for their clothes, another man at the cash register was interested in what was going on. Todd was able to share the love of Jesus with the man at the cash register as well.

After they left the store, Todd found out Jesse was at Guitar Center playing because he had to sell his guitar to pay bail for getting out of prison. He had been clean for a year, but did not have the money to buy any instruments. Todd felt led to buy him a guitar.

So he went back in and bought Jesse the guitar he had always wanted. As they went up to pay, Todd did not need to say anything to the person at that cash register. Jesse actually told the guy at the cash register everything that happened: how Todd had prayed for them, bought clothes for them, talked to them. And because Todd kept pointing out that God had directed him to do these things, Jesse said to the man at the register, "God is buying me this guitar."

I am not sure whether Jesse started a relationship with Jesus that day or not, but the soil of his heart was prepared. Because Todd was willing to listen to God's leading, he was able to participate along with God in soil-building that day.

What opportunities are we missing out on in our lives to be soil-builders? If we were to approach every person we come in contact with a Kingdom mindset, what could happen? Think about how little Todd actually sacrificed and yet he was able to impact someone to possibly change their eternal destiny. Yes, he sacrificed some time, money, and energy, but I'm sure he didn't think of these things as a sacrifice at all.

How does God want you to grow at being a soil-builder? If we are not willing to participate with God in this step, it will be more difficult to take the next step in our seed-life which is to sow seeds. But if we do soil-building correctly, then it prepares the way for us to sow seeds in a proper way. In the next chapter we will discover what this looks like.

REFLECTION QUESTIONS

1. In Mark 4 we read about the Parable of the Soils. The point of the parable is the receptivity of the heart. Do you think about the receptivity of people's hearts around you on a daily basis? Why or why not?

2. In this chapter we talked about tilling the soil. This represented a more aggressive approach to preparing people's hearts to receive the Gospel. Have you or someone you have known tried this approach? How did it work?

3. This type of attitude toward evangelism can often lead to excuses about evangelism in general. What are your greatest excuses for not sharing the Gospel with others?

4. In this chapter it is suggested we take an approach of *soil-building* in regards to our evangelism toward others. How would you define *soil-building* after reading this chapter?

5. Did anything else stand out to you from this chapter?

APPLICATION

1. SACRIFICIAL LOVE – In this chapter, it was suggested that one of the primary ways of being a soil-builder is to exercise sacrificial love. God may want to prune something out of your life to prepare the heart of someone else. Based on the examples given or others you have thought of, what is one thing God is calling you to sacrifice in order to prepare the heart of someone else? Take this step immediately.

2. HEARTFELT QUESTIONS – In this chapter, we discussed using heartfelt questions regarding origin, meaning, morality, and destiny to prepare the hearts of people around us. What is one tangible way you could practice asking more questions?

3. PRAYER – Commit to praying every day for at least one person who needs to have their heart prepared to hear the Gospel. Make sure to watch as God begins to answer your prayers.

Seed Life Spotlight
MINISTERING IN SIOMA
By Sherrill Auker

Journal Entry: 12/20/2015

Sioma continues to confuse me. This culture, these traditions- It is difficult in a new way. We argue about the giving of seed and leave behind disappointed people, unwilling to change.

I know that nothing is impossible with God. I know that He sees the change that is coming. But of all the places I travel in Zambia and DRC, this is the only one that I cannot say, "I'd stay here. This could be my home." Instead, Sioma is always a challenge.

I pray it is not my skepticism returning. More than ever, I feel old mindsets surrounding my ears, pushing to be allowed entrance, to establish roots that dive into my heart. I feel a bit distant. But it is my doing- I am not in the Word- soaking up silence like my heart longs for. I need this week to be set apart, to recapture what has faded. It is not lost - I am new - it cannot change - I will not, cannot, be dead again. I feel the joy, the excitement, the incredible peace deep within - but like trinkets on a barn shelf, they feel dusty. The cobwebs layer and weave around them. They are still within but buried. But if I sit with Him, if I minister to Jesus, settle in the indwelling Spirit, soak in the Word- my Lord will brush off the dust - He will restore these gifts from their soft glow to their original radiance. He is faithful and good. I adore Him. Even in this tired state, He is my treasure and I know He will bring wholeness that I can walk in daily.

The hours travelling to Sioma District, Western Province seemed a premonition of our ministry there. A smooth stretch of pavement merely the precursor to sudden braking, swerving to avoid a car-sized pothole. Every hint of good road seemed a distraction from the tire damage that was to come.

Our team began ministering in Sioma in 2014, connecting with local church leaders and evangelizing through Farming God's Way. Initial meetings were met with apathy, false expectation, and frustration, which attempted to also take root in us.

A local pastor hosted our FGW launch for the region. A group of 25 sat under the shade structure, anticipating announcements of free maize seed and fertilizer gifts. Our lack of either input brought great disappointment. "Sorry, everyone. We bring only education. What we need God has placed in our hands already!" This statement brought skepticism rather than excitement. Halfway through the teaching sessions, we asked, "What time are we teaching until today?"

"We're done learning."

Thinking the attendees must have other responsibilities to tend, Gertrude and I scheduled the demonstration for the following day, packed our supplies, and settled into the vehicle. The rearview mirror showed differently. No one left. The group merely wanted us to stop. Their honesty stunned us, and later became characteristic of the hardness of heart we first encountered in the area.

The next several months brought miscommunication, deceit, manipulation and more from the community. We were spent. And the above journal entry was recorded. Other pages likely rant over the specific chaos we found on trips to Sioma. The Lord does not balk at our openness. Even as this short entry continues, we see how this rejection influenced my state, bringing reevaluation of the heart. Challenges force us to recall the Word and stabilize ourselves on God's promises.

As years passed, we kept returning. We kept sowing. Slowly, we began seeing signs of germination.

Journal entry 3/20/2018

> *Every place we go, I could stay. Western Province was never that way for me. But it seems to be now. Waking up along the river, seeing the progress of leaders that we worked with for several years. There is only potential- where for a while I saw discouragement, now through the patience of an amazing Sector and Sustain team, we're seeing fruit.*
>
> *The Word is effective and powerful. Some seed takes longer to develop, but they do develop- the hard seed coat is worn by the elements and soon the first signs of life appear. A tiny root breaks free, and then the stem pushes its way towards the sky.*
>
> *The Lord fulfills His promises, He seeks out His people. He looks to the one who is humble and contrite in Spirit and trembles at His Word.[54] He is not about mighty buildings or ornate structures- He is the One who created the very matter those are formed from. He is not impressed with grand measures or attempts at constructing a place worthy of His glory. What grabs His attention? Humility. A contrite spirit. A heart moved by His words.*

He isn't looking for incredible sacrifice. He's looking for the one who understands his own identity and God's - and has an appropriate response. When we truly grasp our Father's love and care, when we see that we are His beloved - what other response can there be, but to come in humility, longing for His presence, trembling at His very words.

Years passed, hearts changed - including my own. As we walked in patience and humility, the Lord established the work of our hands and the words of our lips. Ministers in Sioma are living and carrying a powerful message of hope and peace.

Our team ministering in Mwanambao was met with resistance. A typical community meal sparked controversy as attendees mocked Gertrude for not capitalizing on her relationship with foreigners. Though their leaders had previously agreed to provide the staple food for the lunch, no one followed through. Everyone ate the half of lunch we provided, while simultaneously yelling at Gertrude, "How could you come here without mealie meal?! Are you just keeping all the money from the Americans?" The hostility was not quite conducive to learning. But a woman named Eunice was present.

Eunice was the only one from that community who received the message. She tried Farming God's Way, and though she didn't see much success immediately, she was captivated by the Word. We began building a relationship with her, visiting her field and ministering to her family. Together, we walked through family issues and discouragement, each time the effort our team put forth in reaching her home spoke volumes in itself.

Our third year on this journey together, Eunice and her husband Japhet were expecting to attend a leaders' conference hours away. Due to lack of phone reception and deep sandy roads, our detailed invitation did not reach her. Though she didn't know the day or time, the Lord spoke to Eunice, "Don't worry. Someone is coming for you." She wasn't surprised when Saviour and Reuben arrived at the house at midnight, following an 8 hour oxcart ride. They quickly prepared for the journey, but realized she had not soap or items essential for staying away from home. Eunice gave the concern to the Lord and continued finishing laundry.

As they loaded the oxcart headed to the main road, the driver said, "Why don't you use the money you would have spent on this transport for the supplies you need to travel?"

The Lord's faithfulness to Eunice and her family has grounded her. Every concern is answered by His voice. She currently works closely with our missions team, leading Bible studies and ministering in the community, her whole family following the Lord wholeheartedly. A seed sown hit good soil and reaps a harvest.

Unknowingly, we scheduled our training in Lishotokelo during the girls coming of age ceremony. Alcoholism is rampant in communities, but events escalate the issue. Kwibisa, though slightly intoxicated himself, attended our teaching. He alone decided to practice, focusing only on the agriculture aspects and neglecting the spiritual truths woven throughout. Through his rough exterior, we saw a man searching, a lost heart looking for hope.

We invited him to the same leaders conference. Wrestling with demonic influence, he stood in the center of the last evening meeting shouting. We led him outside, a team speaking to him in love. The Word was spoken over his life, and patient ministers quenched the fear that consumed him.

Kwibisa is a changed man. He is overwhelmed by the kindness shown, the grace offered and continues to serve the Lord in his community.

Leaders in this area have risen up to teach others. We met Alex this year, who excels past his faithful instructor, Patrick, a fellow community member. Alex is the first to follow through on a large scale, seeing incredible results in this initial attempt. Large maize cobs during a drought year surprise friends nearby. Patrick has seen his own ability to teach through this harvest, his own capacity to lead others into the potential God has for their lives.

Sioma is fertile ground. The Lord has been seeking His people, sending out faithful ministers to sow seed with a willingness to wait. His eyes are turned towards the one who will, in humility, respond to His Word.

See how the farmer waits for the precious fruit of the earth, being patient about it, until it receives the early and late rains. You also, be patient. Establish your hearts...[55]

No farmer plants seed and expects to reap the following day. The harvest is coming. Keep sowing.

3
Seed-Sowing Part 1
PLANTING THE RIGHT KIND OF SEED

Every Christmas season our mailbox fills up with cards, packages, and my favorite – the annual seed catalog from my favorite company. Because I have ordered from the same company for years, I get a free copy of their full seed catalog. It is a large tome of brightly colored pages, showing off new seeds they have in stock and reminding you of old faithful seeds that have produced well in the past.

I first sit down and look things over once just to see what is new and exciting. Then, over the next several months I sit down more intently with a pen in hand and start to mark up the book. I imagine what kind of garden we will have the next summer and it all begins with the seeds we choose. My wife laughs at me as I pore over the catalog time and time again and explain details about the seeds and plants to her. I understand why she laughs because I get kind of nerdy about the whole process.

When you really think about it, though, seeds are some of the most incredible creations of God. Contained within this seemingly lifeless, tiny shell are the ingredients for life. A seed can be broken into three parts: the embryo, endosperm, and seed coat.[56] The embryo is a multicellular organism, the endosperm is a food source, and the seed coat protects the other two. From these simple ingredients come any number of plants and trees. The whole process is miraculous.

There are two parables of Jesus where He uses the miraculous nature of seeds to describe the Kingdom of God. One is the parable of the growing seed in Mark 4:26-28. Jesus says, "This is what the Kingdom of God is like. A man scatters seed on the ground. Night and day, whether he sleeps or gets up, the seed sprouts and grows, though he does not know how. All by itself the soil produces grain - first the stalk, then the head, then the full kernel in the head."[57] We sow these seemingly innocuous little seeds into the ground and do nothing else except make a suitable environment for it and the seed does its work.

Another famous parable Jesus told about seeds is the parable of the mustard seed. In Mark 4:30-32 it says, "What can we say the kingdom of God is like, or what parable shall we use to describe it? It is like a mustard seed, which is the smallest of all seeds on the earth. Yet when planted, it grows and becomes the largest of all garden plants, with such big branches that the birds can perch in its shade."[58] Although small, seeds have the potential to grow into something huge.

Jesus is using the wonder of seeds to teach us about the wonder of the Kingdom. It is amazing that all we do is put seeds in the ground and the seeds do their work. In the same way, it is amazing that we are called on to sow the seed of life into people around us and God does the work to bring them to life in Him. Just as a mustard seed is so tiny and seemingly inconsequential, so the seed we sow into someone else's life might feel tiny and insignificant. But God can use those tiny seeds to advance His Kingdom in peoples' lives and in the world around us.

In the last section, we talked about our role of working together with God to prepare the soil of peoples' hearts to receive the Gospel. In this section, we will talk about the wonderful privilege of sowing the seeds of the Gospel into peoples' lives.

The concept of sowing seed in people's lives is pretty simple. Basically, God has called us to sow our time, money, energy, actions, and words into the lives of other people to share the "seed of life" or the Gospel with them. As we have talked about so far in this book, God has given us the opportunity to partner with Him to live a seed life, a life devoted to sharing the Gospel with others around us who do not know Him yet.

If sowing seeds in people's lives is so simple, though, why does it seem like such a struggle? As I have talked to people about sharing the Gospel with others, I believe there are some problems keeping them from being effective seed sowers. Either people do sow seed but it does not produce what they thought it would or people find it difficult to sow seed due to fear or guilt. I would like to tackle each one of these problems with the way we sow seed in others' lives and give some insights into how we could be more effective seed sowers.

PROBLEM #1 – Wrong Seed

The first and most alarming problem I have come across is people who are trying to sow seed in other's lives, but are sowing the wrong seed. Often, they think they are doing the right things and in many cases their heart is in the right place. They want people to have a relationship with Jesus and they are out there truly sowing seed. Yet, whether they see it or not, the plant and fruit being produced by that seed is not producing what they hoped it would.

When you plant a seed in a garden or on a farm you have many options of which seed to plant. For example, there are heirloom seeds, which are saved seeds that have been naturally grown and collected for a long time, even centuries. There are hybrid seeds that have been intentionally bred for specific resistance to certain pests and diseases. Then there are also GMO's or Genetically Modified Organism seeds. These GMO seeds are created by taking genetic material from completely different organisms and inserting that genetic material into the seed itself. This process produces seeds that have resistance to certain pesticides and problems. As you plant seeds in your own garden or farm you have to make judgment calls about what particular kind of seed you will be planting.

In a similar way, as we share the Gospel with other people we have to make sure we are planting the right kind of seed because seeds are designed to reproduce in kind. Joel Salatin describes God's design for seeds by saying, "In other words, an apple did not produce a pear. An orchard grass did not produce red clover. Each seed produced true to its parent."[59] So seeds reproduce what is contained within them.

How do we sow the wrong kind of seed? One of the ways that farmers and gardeners develop new hybrid plants is to use a process called "cross pollination." This simply means they intentionally take the pollen of one plant and cross it with another in order to develop a particular hybrid plant that has characteristics of both original plants. This approach has produced some very interesting and reliable vegetables and fruits we buy in the grocery store.

However, in the spiritual sense, there can be a danger to doing this with the Gospel. Sometimes, whether it is because of a philosophical or theological bent, we cross the Truth of the Gospel with another kind of belief or philosophy. Sometimes we do this intentionally, believing that what God desires is the Gospel plus our particular belief or philosophy.

Other times, we do not even know that we are doing it. Anyone who has had a garden for a while has probably seen cross pollination happen even when they were not trying to make it happen. If two perennial plants are open to pollination and an insect cross-pollinates them, the result is a plant that starts to look less and less like the original two plants and more like a cross between the two. In a similar way, we can sometimes unintentionally cross-pollinate the Gospel with something else.

Here are some examples of ways we may cross the Truth of the Gospel with another philosophy or belief:

 *The Gospel AND positive thinking
 *The Gospel AND prosperity theology
 *The Gospel AND politics
 *The Gospel AND cultural relevance
 *The Gospel AND legalistic rules

The list could go on and on. Most of the time I do not think we try to cross pollinate the Gospel with other things.

Yet, we consider these beliefs as so important that when we are sowing the seed of the Gospel into other peoples' lives they do not just see and hear the Gospel. They see and hear the Gospel AND...

This concerns me greatly because it is an impediment to people receiving the Gospel. Even if someone accepts the Gospel it can produce strange fruit in their life. The problem in cross-pollinating plants is that at least initially it can produce some really strange fruit. This past year in our garden we had a plant self-sow that I believe was a cross-pollinated squash. I let it grow because I was interested in what it would look like. When we got to the end of the season, we were left with a white mutant squash that I did not know what to do with. Because we had planted decorative and edible squash plants in the past, I did not know if this one was edible or not and I could not even identify what plant it actually came from. In the end, I just threw it on the compost heap because it was not useful to me as a gardener.

In a similar way, I wonder if this is why we see weak faith in some people. Have we cross-pollinated the Gospel with other philosophies and beliefs to such an extent that it does not produce the fruit God intends?

I recently did counseling with several different people who demonstrated this. As I met with each of them, there was a variation of the same story. They had grown up a Christian, but the Gospel that was passed on to them included legalistic rules which kept them in constant guilt and shame. Decades later, this wrong seed that was sown in their life was producing strange fruit that was keeping them from reaching their full potential in Jesus Christ. So when we sow seed it is important to sow seed that has not been cross-pollinated with anything except the Gospel.

Even more detrimental, though, is seed intentionally designed to be different than the clear Gospel. Without getting into an agricultural debate about whether GMO's are good or bad or whether GMO seed should be used on farms or not, GMO's have some interesting properties that can inform our view of how to sow spiritual seed.

As I said earlier, Genetically Modified Organisms are plants that have been genetically manipulated by companies and scientists. They put selected genetic material from other plants and even animals into a seed for corn or soy or something else and what results is a plant that has interesting capacities. For instance, the company Monsanto, a subsidiary of Bayer, produces GMO's that are resistance to its pesticide product called Round-Up. By genetically altering the seed, the plant produced is resistant to the pesticide even as all of the weeds and other plants around it die.

An interesting wrinkle in the debate about GMO's is that they are specifically designed to not reproduce. Seed and chemical companies are allowed by law to own the genetic composition of their seed. Based on this, they are allowed to put genetic information within the seed that keeps the resulting plant from producing viable seed. This means that instead of a farmer saving seed from the corn he planted the year before, he has to go back to the company each year to buy new seed.

What does this have to do with sowing the Gospel into other peoples' lives? Well, again, without getting into a debate about GMO usage in agriculture, I think GMO's demonstrate the spiritual danger of trying to manipulate the Gospel to our own liking. Sowing the "cross-pollinated" Gospel into other peoples' lives is often unintentional. But there are some who believe strongly that they have to make the Gospel palatable in order for it to be taken seriously.

I have met many pastors, ministry leaders, and churches who instead of declaring the Gospel to people are propagating what I will call in this book "Goals-based Moralistic Opinions." Many of them feel a pressure to avoid talking about sin or sinfulness, avoid mentioning our ultimate eternal destiny, avoid calling people to a complete and utter surrender to Jesus Christ, and avoid confronting cultural norms that are against the way of Jesus. Instead of declaring the Gospel, they are left declaring a message focused on doing better, being a good person, and applying good principles. Some may even try to couch these "Goals-based Moralistic Opinions" in Biblical language. In the end, though, it is like Paul describes in 2 Timothy 3:5, "...having a form of godliness but denying its power."[60]

Even if we are not a pastor or ministry leader, we must be careful to avoid falling into this trap as well. There are many reasons why this is so detrimental, but the greatest one is that it fails the essential test of nature and the Kingdom of God: it does not reproduce. True, vibrant faith in Jesus Christ produces fruit in us that naturally reproduces. But "Goals-based Moralistic Opinions" at best produce half-hearted attempts at following God mixed with plenty of guilt, shame, and cynicism.

I have seen this played out in many different ways in people's lives. Years ago, before becoming a pastor, I started attending a young adult group at a church. It did not take long to realize that many of the people who were there had had "Goals-based Moralistic Opinions" sown into them at some point. The environment was rife with contradictions and hypocrisy. The group talked about the glory of God at their meetings every week but then many of them would party on the weekends. The group talked about God's love and loving other people, all the while demonstrating a deep insecurity and mistrust amongst each other. They bashed churches for not being relevant and loving enough to broken people, while destroying each other's lives by sleeping together, gossiping, slandering, and playing out all kinds of sinful drama.

I am not saying this judgmentally. My heart was broken for the way this group was living out the "Goals-based Moralistic Opinions" they had been taught. What struck me, though, is whether the ministry leader realized it or not, the end result of sowing this "GMO" seed into their lives did not lead to an explosion of Jesus followers. It did not result in miracles and spiritual transformation. Quite the contrary. Despite the continual emphasis on loving people, it led to less truly transformative love. Despite seeking to be relevant it became irrelevant to people who were truly trying to seek God, because it obviously was not working to transform anyone. I had talked to some within the group who actually had people say to them, "Why would I ever follow God if your life looks no different than mine?" Just as GMO seed in the natural world does not reproduce, seed that is simply "Goals-based Moralistic Opinions" will never truly reproduce the life of Christ in someone else.

Before we go on to any other element of being seed-sowers, we must make sure we are sowing the right seed. What does this right seed look like? How do we make sure the seed we are planting is Gospel-centered?

GOD'S AUTHORITY

First, we must make sure the seed we're planting testifies to God's authority. Many times when someone is declaring a cross-pollinated or "GMO" Gospel, the primary reason they felt the need to have a different Gospel was a resistance to God's authority. When God is in authority, there is an absolute Truth and He is the Truth-giver. This means that if God really is in authority, He gets to make the final call on what is right and wrong.

Sometimes, we cross the Gospel with our own opinions because we dislike something God has said or because we are trying to adjust certain truths to better fit into the beliefs of the day. It is like a child who resists the authority of their parent in a decision.

Recently, my four-year-old son disobeyed and I reprimanded him for it. Although he understood he was not to do it again, you could see the gears turning in his mind trying to figure out how to go as far as he could to resist my authority without being obvious about it.

People who try to resist God's authority will only talk about God's love while declaring the Gospel; they will never mention the justice demonstrated by Jesus' death on the cross. They will mention God walking with us in our relationship with Him, but never mention the Bible's declaration that a loving father will also discipline us. They "clean up" the Gospel, removing anything hard or difficult with the resulting message being that coming to Jesus will never actually require us to surrender everything to Him. We can have Jesus AND whatever else we think we need or want.

But the very reason Jesus needed to die on the cross for us was because of our resistance to His authority in our lives. Adam and Eve chose to resist God's instructions and run after their own self-centered desires. The sin in us fights for the same thing. This is why confession and repentance are necessary in our declaration of the Gospel.

In the book "AHA," Kyle Idleman explains how repentance is more than just regretting something that happened in your life. He says:

> *This is the biggest difference between regret and repentance. Many of us will have an awakening and regret that things have turned out the way they have, but we won't repent of our part in it. We regret that someone has noticed and pointed out our wrongs, but we'd rather continue to deceive them and prove ourselves right than actually confess the truth.*[61]

You are not declaring the Gospel of Jesus Christ unless you at some point explain the need to declare that we are wrong and need to turn our backs on our former life. Receiving the Gospel of Jesus Christ means surrender.

How do we sow seed in other peoples' lives that declares this Truth? Obviously, if you get the chance to speak with them about the Gospel you can explain it. But most of the seeds we are able to plant in peoples' lives do not happen in the midst of conversation.

One way to demonstrate God's authority to someone else is to spend time with them but not partake in what they are doing if it crosses the line of God's authority in your life. For instance, if a coworker invites you to join a conversation with other coworkers but it ends up being all about gossip, you can choose to still be there with them but not partake in the gossip. Maybe you believe God has called you to avoid alcohol. You could go to a bar with a friend who invites you but not drink alcohol.

You could also show God's authority in the way you use your money. Using money in a healthy way by getting out of debt and living within your means can show God's authority in your life. Simplifying the things you own and being generous are other ways you could show God's authority. Even what you purchase can show God's authority in your life.

Another way to show God's authority in your life is being willing to confess your sin to others. Sometimes Christians feel as though they should never allow unbelievers to see how they struggle with things. According to Scripture our lives should show less struggle with sin than someone who does not know Jesus, but we will never be perfect. The worst thing we could do when we mess up in front of an unbelieving coworker or friend is to hide it or pretend we did not do anything.

Instead, if we choose to own up to our sins and faults in front of those we have offended, it will be another reminder to them of what we believe about God's authority. By confessing to them and asking for their forgiveness if we have sinned against them, we are showing them we submit to God as our Higher Authority.

These are just a few examples, but for us to sow the Gospel seed into peoples' lives we must believe in God's authority in our lives.

GOD'S GRACE

Another essential element of our communication of the Gospel is the knowledge we are saved by God's grace alone. What distinguishes our faith from every other religion on the planet is God's grace. Ephesians 2:8-10 says, "For it is by grace you have been saved through faith – and this not from yourselves, it is the gift of God – not by works, so that no one can boast."[62]

I explore grace more extensively in my book, *Engage: How to Know God*, if you would like to know how important this is to our faith. Essentially, in other religions a person's salvation is based on the degree to which they perform the commands of their higher power. Only in Jesus Christ do we have a situation where we are saved from our brokenness and sin not because of what we do, but because of God's overwhelming love for us. If we come to Him and surrender our lives to Him, He transforms who we are to allow us to do right things.

If we could earn our own salvation, then it would only be for the elite. Also, it would allow those elite people to boast about their ability to receive salvation while the rest of us could not. Instead, if we believe in faith that Jesus Christ' death and resurrection is our only hope of salvation and we acknowledge our inability to achieve salvation apart from Him, we can receive the free gift of God's grace.

When we are trying to sow the seeds of the Gospel in other people, the importance of this free gift of grace can sometimes get lost. Intentionally or unintentionally we may start to declare God's grace while communicating something different with our behavior.

For instance, I have watched people try to communicate the Gospel to people while also expecting them to jump through several hoops to start a relationship with God. The conversation might go something like this, "God's love and grace are completely free to you if you are willing to come to Him." But we are telling this to a business partner who just watched us berate a waitress for her poor service and give her almost nothing for a tip.

Or maybe you are trying to explain the Gospel to your child. You explain how God's grace is unconditional and covers over every fault, but they have watched your love be completely conditional to them throughout their life. If they behave and follow the rules of the house, then you bestow love and grace. But if they break the rules, then you withhold your love until they fix the problem.

Or maybe you are handing out tracts about God's love to people all the while angrily protesting on the street corner about how wrong a person's lifestyle is. We are declaring that God's grace can cover over the sin of any person, while at the same time putting up a roadblock to conversation by our actions.

When we sow the seeds of the Gospel in someone else's life, we must demonstrate God's grace. One way to do this is to follow Jesus' pattern of going to people instead of expecting them to come to us. Jesus did not wait for us to come to Him. He came to us before we even knew we needed Him. And He did not wait for us to become neat and tidy before He came. He came "while we were still sinners."[63]

In the same way, when we go to people instead of expecting them to come to us we are sowing seeds of the Gospel. And when we choose to act in a spirit of love instead of judgment we are demonstrating God's grace clearly.

Maybe it is intentionally meeting your neighbors when you move into a new neighborhood and taking them a gift instead of expecting them to come to you. Maybe it is looking for the person who is isolated and alone to sit with at lunchtime instead of always going with your friends. Maybe it is intentionally dialoguing with someone who has completely different views than you in a way that does not start conflict but seeks to understand. Maybe it is giving a waiter or waitress who does a poor job an extra tip and writing an encouraging note on your receipt instead of trying to get them fired.

Maybe it is confessing to your kids when you mess up so they understand that Daddy or Mommy needs God's grace as well. Maybe it is being the first to seek reconciliation in a broken relationship. Maybe it is sending a check to someone you know is in need, even if you do not have much yourself. Maybe it is staying late at work without complaint so that someone else can take care of something they need to do.

There are countless ways to demonstrate God's grace in the process of sowing the seeds of the Gospel in their life. It is so important that we get this right though. One of the biggest hindrances to people coming to faith is when we declare something far bigger and more amazing than we demonstrate. If we declare God's grace when we share the Gospel with someone, but our actions do not demonstrate God's grace then why should someone believe us?

God's authority and God's grace are just two of the ways we can make sure we sow Gospel-centered seed. But there are other ways to do this as well. What are some ways that you can make sure to sow the right seed?

REFLECTION QUESTIONS

1. In this chapter we talked about how sowing the wrong kind of seed is one of the main problems we have in sowing the Gospel into people's lives. In nature if we want to produce a certain kind of plant we sow that particular type of seed. If the natural illustration is so simple and straightforward, why do you think we have such a hard time planting the right type of seed in our evangelism?

2. One of the ways we can plant the wrong type of seed is through "cross-pollination." We share a Gospel-AND message with our words and life instead of just the Gospel. Have you seen this in your life at all? Why do you think this cross-pollination happens?

3. In the chapter we also talked about "Goals-based Moralistic Opinions." This seed takes the Gospel and boils it down to principles to be accomplished. We talked about how this kind of "seed" never multiplies like "seed" in the Kingdom should. Have you seen these "Goals-based Moralistic Opinions" in your own life or in others around you?

4. Two hallmarks of true "Gospel Seed" are a clear recognition of God's authority and God's grace. Why do you think these two things are most important to communicate as we are sharing the Gospel with others?

5. Did anything else stand out to you from this chapter?

APPLICATION

1. DEMONSTRATE GOD'S AUTHORITY – Based on the examples in this chapter or others that you think of, choose one way you want to demonstrate God's authority to someone in your life this coming week.

2. DEMONSTRATE GOD'S GRACE – Based on the examples in this chapter or others that you think of, choose one way you want to demonstrate God's grace to someone in your life this coming week.

4
Seed-Sowing Part 2
PLANTING THE RIGHT AMOUNT OF SEED

Another reason we do not see more people coming to know Jesus around us is because we are not sowing enough seed. For some people it is a misunderstanding of what sowing seed really is. If we believe we are only "seed-sowers" if we share a full Gospel presentation with someone, then for many of us that would only be once every couple of months at the most. Some of us have never shared the full Gospel message with anyone.

In this way of thinking, it would be like sowing a seed or two once every couple months. If that was how we handled a garden in real life we would never produce anything. There would be no real garden, just a couple seeds scattered over some soil.

If we want a bountiful harvest, then we need to sow as much seed as we can. In 2 Corinthians 9:6, Paul is speaking to the Corinthians about generosity with their money, but I think the principle he speaks of is applicable here as well. He says, "Remember this: Whoever sows sparingly will also reap sparingly, and whoever sows generously will also reap generously."[64]

Now, salvation is something God does in a person as we have talked about previously. In the end, we cannot cause salvation for someone else just by our actions, but God does invite us into the process. And the principle would make sense that the more seed we sow, the more likely it is that God would use those seeds to produce new life in someone. However, many of us sow very little Gospel-centered seed into other people's lives.

I have talked to many people who look around at the world the way it is and the church the way it is and they get frustrated that the "harvest" is not greater. It feels to them as though their church is not growing, their faith is relatively stagnant, and the community is not being reached the way it needs to be.

The general reaction from most people in this position is to blame the church institution, the pastor, or society for the lack of "harvest." Their focus shifts toward "fixing" the church and making things right so the church can reach more souls. Now, I am not saying that pastors and local churches do not need questions and accountability from the people within the local church. But the church is not a building or an institution. The church is the people within the building.

Blaming the church or a pastor for the lack of "harvest" in a community is like a worker at a farm sitting and drinking iced tea while they complain about the lack of production from the farm. The only way God's kingdom spreads, churches grow, and communities change is when we each take responsibility to sow seed in our circle of influence.

SOWING THE RIGHT AMOUNT OF SEED

How do we sow the right amount of seed? First, we have to remember that seeds come from fruit. If we are not sowing much seed in our life, part of the reason could be we are not producing much spiritual fruit in our life.

Remember the natural process of a seed. Soil is prepared, a seed is planted, it germinates into a seedling, the seedling becomes a plant, the plant produces fruit, and the seeds from the fruit drop onto the soil below it to produce more plants. It is a beautiful process that happens everywhere you look in the wild, whether it is grass, a tree, or a weed.

Jesus focuses on fruit many times in his teaching. In Matthew 7 He describes the difference between true prophets and false prophets. He says:

Watch out for false prophets. They come to you in sheep's clothing, but inwardly they are ferocious wolves. By their fruit you will recognize them. Do people pick grapes from thornbushes, or figs from thistles? Likewise, every good tree bears good fruit, but a bad tree bears bad fruit. A good tree cannot bear bad fruit, and a bad tree cannot bear good fruit. Every tree that does not bear good fruit is cut down and thrown into the fire. Thus, by their fruit you will recognize them.[65]

If we are claiming to follow Jesus, then we should be producing fruit in keeping with our claim that we are walking with God. As Michael Green says about this passage:

A profession of faith that makes no difference to the way we behave is barren and will never save anybody. There must be fruit, consistent, attractive fruit on the tree of our lives. Fruit that will show there is a Gardener at work. Fruit that will satisfy the hunger of the passer-by.[66]

What kind of fruit would this be? Well, in Galatians 5:22-23 it says, "But the fruit of the Spirit is love, joy, peace, forbearance, kindness, goodness, faithfulness, gentleness, and self-control. Against such things there is no law."[67] If we want to sow a good amount of seed through our lives, then we must be producing a good amount of fruit.

Unfortunately, if we were to be truly honest with ourselves, when we look at Galatians 5:22-23 we realize there is not as much fruit in our lives as there ought to be. There could be many reasons for this.

One of the reasons could be because the root of our faith is unhealthy. If a plant does not have a deep root it will not produce much fruit. In a similar way there are some churches and pastors trying to manufacture growth through evangelizing people, but never discipling them. They are usually not doing this intentionally, but they believe God wants them to have a bigger church and the only way they can think of to do that is to make sure everything about their church would be appealing to someone who is not a Christian. We should want to be attractive to someone who is not a Christian. However, the reality is that if we are declaring the true Gospel, there will come a point where our teaching and way of life will deeply conflict with the ways of the world.

Churches who want to side track this in order to avoid tension for people might sow cross-pollinated seed or "Goals-Based Moralistic Opinions" in order to not offend. They scowl at other churches they consider "discipleship" churches believing they are disinterested in reaching people. They say studying the Bible and prayer are nice, but it is more important that they get people trained right away to go out and share the Gospel with others. They believe these "discipleship" churches get so involved with teaching their own people that they never go out and reach unbelievers. In some cases I can understand their frustration, but the whole situation is a false dichotomy.

They believe that if a church focuses on discipleship they do not desire evangelism. But Jesus clearly teaches that life with Him produces fruit, and fruit naturally produces seed. A good "discipleship" church believes that by building up someone in the faith you are naturally preparing them for evangelism with the right seed. The only way for Gospel-centered seed to come from us is to have God do a work in us to produce good fruit.

Maybe you were brought into a relationship with Jesus through a church or ministry like this. Maybe you have been focused on evangelism, but you have been doing evangelism without truly being rooted in your faith with Jesus. If that is the case, then your heart for evangelism is great, but you need to reevaluate the roots of your faith to make sure you are producing good fruit.

On the other hand, maybe you were brought to faith through a different kind of church or ministry. Maybe your church was focused on discipleship, and by discipleship they meant simply training your mind. You went to Bible study after Bible study to gain more intellectual knowledge about God, but that never translated into real fruit in your life and a deep love for people. This would be similar to a garden plant only fueled by one nutrient.

There are three primary nutrients that must be considered in gardening: nitrogen, phosphorous, and potassium. Nitrogen helps a plant produce healthy leaves, phosphorous helps with root growth and fruit development, and potassium allows the functions of the plant to perform correctly.[68] An imbalance of these primary nutrients can affect the growth of the plant. For instance, if there is too much nitrogen and too little phosphorous, there is a chance you could end up with a beautiful looking plant but very little fruit.

This is what happens if you are so focused on growing intellectually in your faith without actually living it out. You invest most of your energy into just one aspect of your spiritual life and it causes you to not produce much fruit. If this is you, you do not need another Bible study right now. You need to practice what you already know.

Perhaps it means taking a break from a Bible study for a season and instead spending that time serving in your church or in a local ministry. Maybe it means meeting up with a friend not only to study but also to talk to God together in prayer and step out in faith to serve others based on what you hear from Him. There are many other ways to take on this challenge.

The point is if we want to produce a good amount of seed in our lives we must be producing a good amount of fruit. So how much fruit is your life producing? Have you come from one of these extremes in your faith or is there something else blocking the way? Are you actively living in sin right now or are you letting the busyness of your world cloud out the work of God in you? If so, we will have limited fruit because we are not giving God space to produce good fruit in us.

KINGDOM POTENTIAL

Another reason we may not be sowing enough seed is because we do not understand the Kingdom potential of every moment of our lives. Every moment we are given is a chance to sow seed. In Ephesians 5:16-17, Paul declares the importance of every moment when he says, "Be very careful, then, how you live – not as unwise but as wise, making the most of every opportunity, because the days are evil."[69] We are to make the most of every opportunity.

Yet, we often miss opportunities. I believe we miss them because we do not understand that every moment has Kingdom potential. What we say, how we act, what we do; everything about our lives communicates something to someone else.

This principle is most clearly taught in Scripture regarding what we say. Proverbs 18:21 says, "The tongue has the power of life and death, and those who love it will eat its fruit."[70] James 3 talks about the power of tongue to destroy if we are not careful. James 3:5-6 says:

Likewise, the tongue is a small part of the body, but it makes great boasts. Consider what a great forest is set on fire by a small spark. The tongue also is a fire, a world of evil among the parts of the body. It corrupts the whole body, sets the whole course of one's life on fire, and is itself set on fire by hell.[71]

That is some strong language, but if you have ever been on the receiving end of destructive words you know the power they hold.

If the tongue does hold the power of life and death, then every word we say to people has potential to draw them toward the Kingdom or hinder their progress toward the Kingdom. Every conversation we have with our kids, our boss, the lady at the coffee shop, the man who cut in line at the grocery store, and every other person we meet on a daily basis is a chance to either draw or hinder, give life or give death.

How many of us disconnect our faith-filled conversations and conversations at church from the other words we speak throughout our week? But there has never been a moment in your life that your words were not important. Every word you say and also how you say those words either draws someone toward the Kingdom or hinders their progress toward the Kingdom.

This is also true with our actions, not just our words. Every action you take toward someone can draw or hinder. There is kingdom potential in every moment. When we recognize this, it expands our vision for what this life is truly all about. I often have conversations with people who see Christianity as boring. They do not see the adventure that faith is: walking with God and being a co-worker in the Kingdom. I believe they see faith as boring because they are viewing their faith journey as if they are passive passengers on the journey of faith. They are simply hanging out and hanging on as God drives them toward eternity with Him.

Before I got a drivers' license I was required to have a permit for six months. I could only drive if my parents or an adult were driving with me. Before this point in my life, I was only a passenger, looking out the window and day-dreaming as someone else drove me to my destination. When I got my permit, however, I was no longer a passenger. I had responsibility.

I remember when this reality dawned on me. I was helping to drive back from a family trip at a point in southern

Pennsylvania where the highway went over mountains. It was getting late and everyone had dozed off. I had been driving under my permit for a long time and I felt confident I did not need to wake anyone up. But then the mountain pathway seemed worse than I remembered. Fog rolled in and it was hard to see. For the first time it dawned on me that when I was in the driver's seat I had my family's lives in my hand.

Now, as a husband and father of two little boys I take on this responsibility every time we travel. What if one day I said, "I have made sure to be responsible with my driving every single day I am out on the road with my family. Today, I am not going to pay attention. Today, I am just going to let go of the steering wheel and see where the car takes us." You would think I was the worst husband and father imaginable. Why? Because I have a responsibility and if I chose to let go of that responsibility for even a second on the road my family could literally die.

How does this connect with the Kingdom potential of every moment? We must always remember that salvation is God's work and not ours. But too often we just imagine ourselves as passengers in our faith. We assume we just need to sit back and relax and let God take us where He wants to go. But God is a gentleman; He is not going to take you somewhere you do not want to go. He is the one that leads, but He puts the responsibility in our court to follow Him.

What if we are like a driver with a permit? Our Heavenly Father is sitting there directing and guiding us on our journey, but we have the responsibility to utilize the Kingdom potential He has given us in each moment of our lives. This would definitely change our sense of responsibility and adventure in our faith, wouldn't it?

Basically, there is a moment that needs to happen in each one of our lives (and if you have never had this moment I pray it happens right now) where we become frustrated enough with our faith journey to know something needs to change. We realize we are not really taking responsibility for our part of God's Kingdom work. We are frustrated that there are people dying daily who are going to be eternally separated from God and it seems as though so few people are coming to know God. We wish God would let us be more a part of the process. Then it dawns on us that He is not stopping us from being more a part of the process. We have been standing there with seed in our hands the whole time, just not choosing to scatter it. We finally realize the Kingdom potential of every moment we have been missing out on.

When this happens, we start to realize that dining out at a restaurant is not just dining. It is a chance to bless a waiter or waitress with a smile, a really good tip, or a heartfelt question. Holidays with our extended family are not just a chance to sit, eat, and have family drama. It is a time to serve, to listen, to challenge. Our gym time is not just "me-time," but a time to pray, to encourage, to witness. Our time with our family is not just about survival, but it is about planting seeds in our children that move them on to salvation and holiness. We start to sow seed constantly because it is our life. We start to truly engage every person, every day, with a Kingdom mindset.

So why don't we just do this naturally? Why does it take an awakening to realize the Kingdom potential of every moment? Because it takes sacrifice. It takes a willingness to say my life is not my own at all. It is all about Jesus. Many of us want to follow Jesus wholeheartedly and give Him our entire lives, but we make the excuse that things always get in the way of us living the life we know we should live. But the longer we wait to submit everything to Jesus and understand the Kingdom potential of every moment, the less effective our seed-sowing will be.

I have purchased some seeds over the years that I planned to sow, but I got too busy with other things to sow them. What happens over time is the germination rate of those seeds goes down. Maybe at first they would germinate at ninety-five percent, but if I keep holding onto them and not sowing them there will come a time that almost none of them will germinate even if I did sow them.

In a similar way, if we keep waiting and holding onto a wrong picture of our lives of faith, we will be waiting there with a handful of seed that even if sown will lose its likelihood to germinate. We will have missed so many opportunities that the few opportunities we do take will be less likely to lead to a truly transformed life for another person.

Our lives are not our own. We were created by and for God and our entire lives are His to use as He pleases. In 1 Corinthians 6:19-20 it says, "Do you not know that your bodies are temples of the Holy Spirit, who is in you, whom you have received from God? You are not your own; you were bought at a price. Therefore, honor God with your bodies."[72] In the original context this was Paul speaking to the Corinthians about sexual purity. But I think it points out a deeper biblical principle as well. Our lives are not our own; God's grace, through Jesus' death and resurrection, bought us back from sin and death. We are traveling temples of the living God, who is at work in and through us. We were meant to have a seed-life and be seed-sowers. If this is true, then we must honor God with every word, action, and attitude we have.

NOT ALWAYS PLEASANT

If we were bought at a price and meant to have a seed life, then we must also acknowledge the fact that not all of our seed-sowing will be pleasant. Sometimes, we sow too little seed because we get so focused on our own problems in difficult seasons to think about sowing seed in other peoples' lives. Instead of continuing our perspective of having a seed life and being seed-sowers, we start to focus all of our attention on people taking care of us and having their attention on us.

Now, I am not saying it is wrong to let others take care of us. We should be helping each other in the body of Christ. The problem comes when we get so entangled in our own problems, struggles, and unpleasant situations that we miss the opportunities God has given us.

In nature, there are three main ways God designed seeds to be distributed. One way is through animals, a second way is through ocean or fresh water, and the third primary way is by wind.[73] Think about that third way for a second: the wind. If you were a tree that was designed to distribute its seed through wind, when do you think would be an ideal time for seed distribution? Probably during a storm when the wind is at its height.

Now, think about this in terms of our lives. If in nature, God made it so that some plants are best sown in storms, don't you think the same would be true for us spiritually? Sometimes, the only way for people to see Jesus in us is for Him to take us through difficulty. Pain was not God's intention from the beginning of time. He created Adam and Eve to walk with Him and be at peace. But pain is part of our daily lives here and now due to sin and death. And that means we will go through difficult times in our lives, but thankfully, God has a knack for bringing beauty out of brokenness.

If we try to resist God in those difficult seasons of our life we will not find healing from our sorrow. Beyond that, we will at best miss opportunities to sow seed in other peoples' lives and at worst sour the soil of others' hearts so that they do not want to hear about God. But, if by God's grace, we trust God in the midst of those difficult seasons, it can become an ideal time to sow seed in the lives of other people.

A friend of mine, Andrew, lost his brother in an unfortunate accident a few years ago. I remember thinking how hard this time would be for his family. His brother was young and had many years ahead of him it would have seemed. But Andrew's faith astounded me.

To him, as much as he needed to grieve his brother's passing and be with his family during this time, he also felt a deep need to not waste this time. More than anything else, he wanted to make sure his grief did not overshadow the chance to share the Gospel with all kinds of people who might not otherwise hear it.

He wanted the funeral to be a time to honor his brother, but he also wanted the Gospel to be clearly shared. Andrew told me story after story of opportunities he would get to share the hope He had in Jesus during this time with other people. He bought dozens of books to hand out to people he was sharing the Gospel with and conversations continued to happen months after his brother's death.

Andrew recognized God had a right to use his life to share seed with other people, even if it had to come through a "windy storm." He trusted God, knowing God loved him dearly, but he also loved other people that might never get another chance to hear the Gospel. One of the reasons we might not be sharing enough seed is because we do not have this perspective. Hard times leave us close-fisted with sharing seed, instead of realizing that God may want to use those difficult times for His glory.

CONCLUSION

So one of the major problems we face in being seed-sowers, other than sowing the wrong seed, is that we do not sow enough seed. We talked about several reasons why this happens in our lives. In order to be effective seed-sowers and live a seed-life, we must remember a couple key things.

First, we must remember that seeds come from fruit. If our spiritual lives are not producing fruit, then we will never sow the amount of seed we should be sowing.

Second, we must understand the Kingdom potential of every moment. Every word, action, and attitude is a chance to draw someone toward the Kingdom or hinder their progress. When we understand this, then having a seed-life makes sense. Every moment is a chance to sow a seed.

Third, we must remember that God may choose to use you to sow seed into someone else's life even if it doesn't feel good. Sometimes, the most difficult situations in our lives are the most ideal times to sow seed in other people's lives. If we understand these three concepts we will be on a good track to be sowing the right amount of seed in peoples' lives.

REFLECTION QUESTIONS

1. When you do not see much of a spiritual harvest in your church or community, do you find it easier to blame the church or church leadership instead of looking at yourself? Why do you think this is easy to do?

2. One of the main reasons we do not sow enough seeds is because we do not produce much fruit in our spiritual lives. Do you believe your life is producing spiritual fruit? One of the ways you can tell is if the things happening in your spiritual life are impacting other people's lives.

3. One of the main points of this chapter (and also of this book) is the Kingdom potential of every single moment of our lives. Every word we say and everything we do can have an impact on getting someone closer to the Kingdom. Is it hard to remember this Kingdom potential in your life? Why or why not?

4. One of the ways God uses us to sow the seed of life in other people is through difficult seasons. Seed in nature is often distributed through storms. In the same way, God may use a storm in our life to share the Gospel with someone else. Have you seen this in your own life or someone else's life?

5. Did anything else stand out to you from this chapter?

APPLICATION

1. EVALUATE – Pray and ask the Lord to identify how you may not be producing as much fruit as you should.

2. REMEMBER – Determine this week to remind yourself of the Kingdom potential of every moment. Whether it means setting an alarm on your phone or putting a note in a conspicuous place, do whatever it takes to remind yourself that there is Kingdom potential in every moment.

3. LOOK UP – If you are going through a difficult time right now, ask God to give you His perspective of the situation.

Seed Life Spotlight
STORIES OF KINGDOM POTENTIAL
By Sherrill Auker

"What is your current average corn yield per acre?"

The conference attendees look around, waiting for the first person willing to submit an answer. Average yields for Southern and Western Provinces of Zambia are 11% of their potential. Loss and crop failure are deemed normal. The responses of the group are rarely encouraging. This basic needs assessment, the discovery of the current harvest situation, soil issues, and seasonal activities always closes with the same question.

"Is this what God intends for you?"

Are the low yields, the soil erosion, the rainfall runoff the best scenario? Are these frustrations and disappointments that we've known our whole lives really it?

I've never had a group reply, "Yes."

A seed of hope has already been planted. Solomon tells us the Lord "has put eternity into man's heart."[74] The aching of *there's more* lives in every person. Meant to bear the image of God, individuals are living with a missing piece. But a seed is present - even in the most unexpected places, where no evidence exists.

Joe and Pronella are leading in the transformation of their community in Mapanza Chiefdom. Six months ago, their lives were turned upside down by a short-term evangelistic team willing to sow seed in unlikely soil.

Joe was a known alcoholic, with multiple girlfriends. His wife, though hurt and frustrated, remained with him, caring for their children. When the short-term team arrived, Joe was one of the first to hear the message. He followed the team around for a time, impacted by the Word of God. Before long, he accepted Christ and walked house to house with the team, soaking up the Word. As the week continued, Joe began sharing the Word of God himself, encouraging other community members to experience the same life change he had.

Others followed suit, leaving behind their past and becoming new in Christ. Pronella became suspicious regarding Joe's touring with the foreigners, assuming he'd find another woman to replace her. As his life-change continued and his passion for evangelism grew, she left him.

Our team returned to the community the next month, following the expedition team with an agricultural discipleship program. When we arrived, Joe was waiting for us at the campsite. A two-hour impromptu Bible study broke out as we responded to his enthusiastic questions. Eventually, he returned home, anxious for our evening revival meeting.

Joe arrived early - with Pronella. She had returned home that very day, an answered prayer. The group gathered around the campfire, sang praise choruses and listened to the gospel message. Pronella received Christ and healing as the team prayed over her. Joe came forward with her, believing for full reconciliation with his wife.

Within three months, this couple attended our leaders conference, gaining a bigger perspective for God's work in their nation. They returned home with an even greater passion for the Lord and the ministry. Currently, they lead transformation in their community, guiding evangelistic efforts and Bible studies. New believers capable of prompting incredible change because of the imperishable seed planted within them.

...You have been born again, not of perishable seed, but of imperishable, through the living and abiding word of God; for "All flesh is like grass and all its glory like the flower of grass. The grass withers, and the flower falls, but the word of the Lord remains forever." And this word is the good news that was preached to you.[75]

When change occurs through the Holy Spirit, the past is gone, and a new life is born. Joe doesn't fear the recurrence of alcoholism; Pronella is able to forgive and offer grace. The Word of God has been planted in their lives and remains, forming a new foundation that their lives are built upon.

The Word is powerful. As believers, we are asked to sow the Word, even when a situation doesn't feel like it holds much promise.

After preaching an introductory meeting in a new chiefdom, I asked people to come forward for prayer. The group was unresponsive to the message, seemingly apprehensive of our team. But several came forward. The atmosphere was awkward, distracting, but we pressed through and spoke life into each individual who asked for prayer. We saw the Lord work, freeing people of pain and struggle, but the feeling that *more should be happening* held fast.

"Will you come pray for my son?" Hilton led us along rocky paths to his home and called his son outside. Jimmy, in obvious pain, walked over to us with head down. For weeks, his hand had been swollen to twice the normal size. Sleep was impossible for him, the ache causing restless nights. The pain was so significant, he couldn't even speak to us. We prayed for him, reassuring him with the promises of God and encouraged him to speak the Word over his own life. As we left, we told him: "When we come back, we're going to greet you with a handshake."

Two weeks later, we did. The swelling began to decrease the very day we had prayed for him. Mobility returned, and Jimmy fully recovered. Seeing God's faithfulness stirred up a hunger for a true relationship with Him.

The evening revival meeting we held upon our return was the *more* we had believed was coming. Over 50 received Christ and many were delivered from strongholds in their lives.

Jimmy was a first-fruit of the community. Though the situation was grim, the sowing of the Word in faith reaped a harvest. One never knows how far a seed will travel, how far the ripple effect will spread when a stone is thrown in a calm lake.

Their third day of ministry, an expedition team to Cambodia arrived in a certain village. They shared the gospel with an older lady and her adult son at her home. After the team prayed for the mother's sore throat, the son requested prayer for his daughter with Downs syndrome who was unable to speak. After the team prayed, she started speaking! He accepted Christ immediately. That evening, spirits attacked him at night. Confident of his new authority in Christ, he sent them away in the name of Jesus.

The man then took the team next door to another family member's house. The new believer's sister was chained up, believed to be mad. As the team ministered to her, she accepted Jesus. The ripple effect continued as they met her son upon leaving the house. After sharing with him, he also accepted Jesus. That evening, the chained woman had her first peaceful night in four years, and the drastic change prompted her older sister to receive Christ!

The spirits returned to the first man's house the following night. He was sleeping, but his wife was afraid, greatly affected by them. She woke him up, and he immediately sent them away in the same manner as before. She received Christ as a result of seeing the power of the Holy Spirit.

The grandmother, her three children, and one's wife, and a grandchild had all accepted Christ in a two-day span! The team sowed seed that multiplied quickly!

Kingdom potential lives in every moment. If we sow without fear, stepping out in faith believing in the Word's power, a harvest will follow. The gospel is enough to redeem and transform lives. There is *more* promised to us, *more* available to us, *more* to be expected as the Word goes out. We can be confident sowers, knowing the one who causes germination is always present, always at work. Our role is the distribution of seed in love, wisdom, and persistence, knowing the Grower is always faithful to see it through.

5
Seed-Sowing Part 3
PLANTING SEED IN THE RIGHT PLACE
AND AT THE RIGHT TIME

A final problem we can have in being effective seed-sowers is sowing seed in the wrong place or at the wrong time. As I have grown in my understanding of gardening, it became much more obvious to me how important it is to know the right season and soil conditions a particular seed or plant requires before you plant it. You can plant the right kind of seed and the right amount of seed, but still struggle because you did not consider the season and conditions.

When I first began gardening, I would plant all kinds of crops I thought would be good to eat. I had heard someone say not to plant things outside until Memorial Day since we live in the northeast, so I waited until then and sowed all of the seed I had. Some things did really well. Other things did not do well at all. At the time I was confused what would have made the difference. Looking back now, I can see the seeds and plants that did not do well did poorly because they were planted out of season or planted in the wrong conditions.

Vegetables like carrots, beets, spinach, lettuce, potatoes, onions, peas, and kale all love being started in cool weather. In fact, some crops like peas are said to taste significantly better if it snows as they are germinating. For many of these plants, if you plant them out once it starts to get warm they are either not going to germinate at all, or they are going to do poorly once they do germinate. Many of these plants I now put out as soon as the soil is not frozen anymore.

There are other seeds and plants that would never germinate or would actually die if I tried to plant them in cool weather. Beans, squash, cucumbers, basil, tomatoes, peppers, and eggplants all like the warm weather. If you try to plant out these seeds or seedlings in the cool weather they are going to struggle. You have to wait until you are sure there will be no chance of frost before you would even consider planting these out.

Beyond the importance of planting with the seasons is soil pH. PH is the measure of how acidic or alkaline a particular patch of soil is. Soil of around seven on the pH scale is right in the middle between acidic and alkaline. If the soil is lower than seven then it is acidic. If it is higher than seven it is alkaline. Most plants like the soil to be right around neutral or a little acidic. But there are other plants that can only grow well in very acidic soils. For instance, blueberries, azaleas, and rhododendrons require acidic soils.[76] If you try to plant these into neutral or slightly alkaline soils at best they would struggle and at worst they would not grow at all.

What does this have to do with being effective seed-sowers? I think pH and seasons teach us a lot about why even when we do sow the true Gospel into other peoples' lives and we sow enough seeds on a regular basis, it seems to not be effective at bringing about new life in people. If we are not sensitive to sowing seed at the right time and in the right place, then we will find very few of the seeds we sow will germinate.

THE pH OF THE HEART

Let's start by looking at the pH of the heart. We must recognize as we are sowing seed that each person is an individual and every person's story is a little bit different. This is what gives me pause when I see someone take one method of evangelism and try to use it in every situation. It is like having a hammer and trying to use it for every project. We must remember that every person has a story and every person's preparedness to receive the Gospel is different.

You might say, "This sounds a lot like the section on preparing the soil of the heart," and it is. But the pH of the heart has more to do with choosing the right way to sow the seed instead of preparing the soil itself. You might say that someone's past experiences, personality and learning style, mental resistance to the faith, and their current situation form the pH of their heart. If we have an idea of the pH of their heart, it helps us know the right way to sow seed into their life.

For instance, say you have a friend who has been hurt by a church before. Maybe it was a church where they declared big things about God but lived very hypocritical lives. Maybe it was a legalistic church that did not show much love. Maybe a pastor had a moral failing. Maybe because of someone's background, people in a church judged them and did not allow them to truly become a part of the community.

If this is the case, then your first step in sowing seed in their life is most likely not going to be inviting them to your church. They already do not trust "the church." Instead, maybe the way to sow seed in their life is to simply love them and show them that not all Christians are like the ones they came in contact with previously.

Or maybe based on personality, physical issues, or life circumstance someone is relationally needy. They are the type of person that takes extra love to be around. I sometimes refer to people like this as "special friends." Sometimes they are a special friend because they are socially awkward and do not know how to interact with people. Or maybe they were raised in a very abusive or destructive home and it means they are living out severe emotional wounds.

If this is the case, do you think it would work to sow the seed of the Gospel once and then expect them to respond to it? God can do anything, but what I have found is that many of these people have had people come and go in their life. For them to hear the Gospel it usually takes a consistent, demonstrated Gospel love shown over a period of time in their lives.

Or maybe someone has a mental resistance to faith. They are struggling with doubts about some fundamental scientific and philosophical questions about faith. I get so frustrated when I watch other believers either judge people who have questions or just tell them "it's all about faith." I was this person for a part of my life, and it is not a bad thing to have questions and doubts as long as you are willing to search for the Truth.

But if someone is truly looking for the answers to these questions and another person's action of sowing seed in their life is to say, "Don't worry about those questions because it's all about faith," then they are misjudging the condition of their heart. Instead, what if they truly listened to their concerns and pointed them to helpful resources? This might be a better way to sow seed in their life.

There are many other examples. A shy personality, someone overwhelmed or depressed, or the level of someone's education. Now, am I saying that if God tells you to sow a seed in someone's life who might seem to go against these examples, that you should go against His will? By no means. Sometimes, He will call us to share the Gospel in ways that do not make sense. But at the same time, just as God designed pH in the soil, I think He wants us to be discerning about the pH of someone's heart.

During college, I would take on various summer jobs. One summer, I worked at a cookie factory. It was a very unique job. I never thought the smell of cookies could ever get old, but it definitely does when you smell like a cookie for an entire summer. I had many interesting adventures working at that factory.

The first couple weeks I was there I was given the entry level job. Basically, there was a conveyor belt with hundreds if not thousands of cookies coming at you every minute towards a packaging area. My job when I first started was to stand with a stick next to the packaging area watching and waiting for cookies to get stuck. If they did get stuck, I was to use my stick to break up the cookies that were clogging the process and get things back in working order. It was relatively mind-numbing after a while. I would work between 8-12 hours a day watching cookies and if things did not get clogged then I literally just stood there all day.

The nice thing was I had a partner at this station. This meant I had someone to have a conversation with and if God gave opportunity possibly sow some seeds of the Gospel. I was excited about this opportunity until I started talking to my partner. If I remember correctly his name was Jorge, and Jorge did not like me very much. Sometimes, out of spite, when a cookie got clogged on his side he would just stand there and look at me until I reached over the conveyor and unblocked his side as well. He would also occasionally just stare at me with a hateful look.

It threw me for a little bit of a loop. I could not figure him out. All I had done was try to talk to him and get to know him. Now, there were a lot of forces against the possibility of me sowing seed in his life. First, it was a very loud factory and we were on opposite sides of the conveyor. Second, there were some cultural and language barriers. But I did not find out about the third and most important barrier until later.

At one point during our conversations I had told him I was studying to be a pastor. He did not tell me right away, but he finally came clean with why he disliked me so much. One day he told me that pastors only get into the ministry for the money. This confused me because where I came from I knew the vast majority of pastors got paid below or far below the average income of the area they lived in. I had grown up in a pastor's household and for many of those years my dad was well taken care of by the churches he served at. But at the first church he pastored, my parents were barely making enough money to put food on the table. It was more common for us to hear about pastors that could barely make it financially versus ones that were given an excessive wage.

I knew the truth was that the vast majority of pastors were not in it for the money. I could have taken Jorge's comments as offensive in some way and I could have tried to convince him otherwise. Or I could have ignored his comment completely and continued to try to sow the message of the Gospel into him through our conversations. If I did either of those things, though, I would be ignoring the pH of his heart.

There must have been some circumstance that shaped Jorge's opinions about pastors. Whether it was a pastor who was greedy or a pastor who embezzled money or a televangelist that Jorge watched who always talked about money or wealth, it must have driven him to the conclusion that all pastors wanted was money. His heart was predisposed to ignore pastors because he thought they were always looking for money.

If I was to be an effective seed-sower in that situation, I would have needed a sensitivity to the pH of his heart and then sown seed accordingly. Jorge and I got moved to different places before I could have a significant amount of time to sow seed into his life. But, if I had more time, maybe I could have done things like be generous with my words, time, energy, and money to show him that his perception of pastors and God might be wrong.

For instance, instead of having the conversation focus on me I could have intentionally focused most of the conversation on him. If he would have kept staring me down and making me work his side of the conveyor belt as well, I could have done it without complaining. Maybe I could have blessed him with a gift card for being my coworker. Whatever the case, I would be praying for God to give me wisdom for the best way to sow seeds that would accommodate the pH of his heart.

Everyone we come in contact with has a slightly different pH of their heart. Some are more resistant to seed-sowing than others. For some, it might take years of seed-sowing to the pH of their heart before they are willing to accept the Gospel. For others, it might not take so long. Either way, it is so important that we think about the pH of someone's heart as we are sowing seed.

SEASONS

As important as the pH of someone's heart is, knowing the season that someone is going through is just as important. The King James Version of Isaiah 50:4a says, "The Lord God has given me the tongue of the learned, that I should know how to speak a word in season to him that is weary..."[77] Proverbs 25:11 says, "A word fitly spoken is like apples of gold in a setting of silver."[78] There is a clear biblical principle that we should watch how we say things depending on the season someone is going through.

For instance, maybe someone is going through a time of grief because of the loss of a loved one. It would be insensitive of us to completely ignore this grief in someone's life and "charge in" trying to sow seed that would not take this into account. Romans 12:15 says, "Rejoice with those who rejoice; mourn with those who mourn."[79] We are instructed by Scripture to minister to someone according to their season. Maybe sowing seed looks different to someone grieving. How can I grieve with them? What could I supply that would encourage them? How could I show the Gospel with my life more than try to convince them of the Gospel?

Or maybe someone is at the completely opposite level. Maybe the person you are thinking of is at the top of their game: great job, busy schedule, wonderful family, with not a care in the world. Sowing a seed into this person's life by trying to tell them how God can lift up the struggling and the needy might not make sense to them. Instead, maybe because of the season of their life you could ask heartfelt questions about whether all their success has truly satisfied the deepest questions in their life of meaning, morality, and destiny.

We must "watch the weather" in the lives of people around us and listen to God as He guides us in the best times and ways to sow seed into their lives. Sometimes God gives us direct insight into these things. Other times, He just sets up circumstances to be able to make seed-sowing possible.

We have a dear friend, Holly, who came to know Jesus through the college ministry I previously led. The first night she ever came to our ministry was an interesting experience. For the college students, we would have a normal weekly gathering that included teaching, worship, and small groups, but we also occasionally had other unique nights where we played games or did a service activity.

One night, around Christmas time, we had a service night wrapping gifts and preparing things for AngelTree, a ministry that helps the children of incarcerated people get presents during the Christmas season. We were excited to be part of this ministry and we thought we had things relatively prepared, but the night felt like chaos. Many people could not wrap gifts well, certain special friends were being relationally needy, and things just seemed out of control. This just happened to be the night that Evan, who had attended our college ministry for a while, decided to invite Holly to come.

We did not get to talk to Holly as much as we hoped that night. Because of the chaos of things, we doubted whether she had a good experience and would want to come back to check out a "normal" night. But, it just so happened that Holly was a world traveler and loved helping people of all places and backgrounds. And in the season of life she was in she had a void of true community and answers to questions she had about life and God. She thought it was cool that a group like ours was serving people we did not even know. Even though it was chaotic, seeing the Gospel in action through service met her in the right season of her life.

Would she have stayed if it was a different season of her life? I'm not sure. Would she have been open to the message of the Gospel if it was just a normal night with teaching and worship? I'm not sure. But, God saw it fit to have this night be the night she first attended our group.

From that point forward Holly continued to attend our group and learn more about the Gospel. She surrendered her life to God and has been pursuing Him faithfully since then. And she has gotten the chance to sow seeds of life in many other lives. Several years after surrendering her life to Jesus she went on a missions' trip to Haiti. While there, she got stung by a bee and it started an autoimmune reaction in her body. Years followed of serious health issues and brought her close to death.

Her local community rallied around her and we also were able to start a GoFundMe campaign to raise money for her to go to the Mayo Clinic. Finally, she was diagnosed and was able to stabilize the autoimmune reaction in her body called Dysautonomia. It was terrible to watch her go through this. But, she was able to use this season of her life to sow the seeds of the Gospel in many other people's lives. She was a testimony of God's grace during this time and others started a relationship with God because of watching God at work in her.

This all started with God setting up the right environment and season in her life for her to first accept that seed of the Gospel into her life. All God calls us to do is to be sensitive to the pH of someone's heart and the seasons of life they are going through. When we do this, it makes us effective seed-sowers.

CONCLUSION

The section of the book about seed-sowing is the longest. The reason is that effective seed-sowing is essential to having a seed life. Effective seed-sowing means we are sowing the right seed, in the right amount, at the right time, and in the right place. In nature, when you sow the right seed, in the right amount, at the right time, and in the right place it is amazing how quickly and prolifically seeds can germinate and grow. In a similar way, although it is God who brings someone to life and not us, if we are faithful to sow the right seed, in the right amount, at the right time, and in the right place there is a greater chance of someone responding to the Gospel. Just like Holly's story, the multiplication of that seed can be incredible.

I recently heard a quote that said something like this: "In every seed a tree, and in every tree a forest."[80] This should encapsulate for us the power of a seed life. In nature, inside each tree seed is the potential for a tree. For some seeds, the tree it produces is ten, fifty, or even hundred feet tall, and that tree contains all the seed it needs to produce a forest over time.

As we become more effective at sowing seeds, remember we are not just sowing a seed or even a tree. If God is involved, for every seed we sow He may be sowing a forest.

REFLECTION QUESTIONS

1. The main issue this chapter tackles is sowing seed in the wrong place and at the wrong time. Have you or someone you've known ever tried to sow seed into someone's life at the wrong place or the wrong time? How did that work out?

2. It is helpful to understand the pH of someone's heart – how they will react to the Gospel based on their past experiences, their current situation, and their overall worldview. On a scale of 1-10, how effective do you think you are at understanding the pH of someone's heart? How could you get better at this?

3. Understanding the season someone is going through is also important to the process of sowing seed. On a scale of 1-10, how effective are you at being sensitive to the season someone is in when you are talking to them? How could you get better at this?

4. This anonymous quote was referenced at the end of the chapter: "In every seed a tree, and in every tree a forest." What is your reaction to this quote? How would it change your perspective if this is how you viewed your life?

5. Did anything else stand out to you from this chapter?

APPLICATION

1. THE pH LIST – Write down a list of people you know who do not know Jesus yet. Maybe they are names you

have been thinking about throughout this book. Next to each name write down what you know about their past experiences, their current situation, and their overall worldview. What might God want you to do with this knowledge? How might He want you to adjust the way you are sowing seed in their life?

2. SEASONS – Consider the season that different friends, family, or coworkers might be in right now. Ask the Lord to give you insight into a way to bless them specifically in this season.

6

Son-Sharing
PROVIDING THE RIGHT ENVIRONMENT FOR THE SEED

Merriam Webster defines the word "environment" as "the circumstances, objects, or conditions by which one is surrounded."[81] The health of something is often dictated by its environment.

For instance, if you have a fish in the water, an environment it was designed to live in, it can be happy and healthy. But the instant you lift that fish out of the water it starts to die. Why? Because the environment it was designed to live in is water. This is relatively obvious.

However, even when something is in the environment it was designed to live in, there are so many environmental factors that can still be a little bit off. If these factors are off significantly enough and for a long enough time period, it can hinder or completely destroy the chance for life.

Consider pregnancy. One study found that when you factor in unknown miscarriages, a woman was just as likely to miscarry a pregnancy as she was to have a pregnancy go to full term.[82] The environment of the womb and the processes leading to the baby developing well have to be in perfect harmony for a pregnancy to come to term.

Or consider our planet. When many scientists talk about Earth's environment they discuss the Goldilocks Principle.[83] Basically, if you look at Venus, Earth, and Mars they are very similar to the story of Goldilocks. Venus is too close to the sun and too hot. Mars is too far away and too cold. Earth is in the exact position it needs to be to sustain life as we know it. God has designed our planet to be the perfect environment necessary for our survival.

In a similar way we must consider whether the environmental factors of someone's life are an ideal place for the seeds of the Gospel to grow. So far in this book, we have talked about the preparation of the soil through soil-building. There is a preparation aspect necessary in someone's heart before the seed of the Gospel is planted. Healthy soil provides the right environment for a seed to be planted.

Then, we talked about the actual act of sowing seed in someone's life. Many things can go wrong in our attempts to sow seed in other peoples' lives. We must work together with God to sow seed in the proper way.

But, even if we have carefully worked together with the Lord to prepare the soil of someone's heart and sow seed properly, we can still see a lack of harvest or actual transformation in someone's life. This could be because we are not considering the best environmental factors within which that seed can grow.

When I first started gardening I would buy tomato and pepper plants at a local garden center because it takes a long time to start them yourself. If you are going to get strong and healthy tomato and pepper plants ready to be sown in May or June you need to start seeds indoors in March. Previously, I did not have the equipment or the knowledge to do this effectively.

In the past two years I finally got some equipment that would allow me to start seeds indoors. I decided to give it a shot. Tomatoes were relatively easy for me to grow, but I had heard pepper seeds could be notoriously finnicky about germinating. They were particularly sensitive to temperature since they are a warm weather plant. The first year I tried to germinate them I don't think I had a single one survive. This past year I had around thirty seedlings survive that I was able to plant out.

Here's the point. When I first started to grow peppers inside, I had really good soil for them to grow in and I planted the seeds properly in specially designed containers and a good amount of moisture. However, I forgot the environmental factor most important to that pepper plant's germination: heat. The reason I had good germination the second year was because I invested in a warming mat that the soil could sit on. It heated the soil where the pepper plants were and sure enough the pepper seeds that I planted started to germinate. One environmental change and the seeds I planted went from dead to thriving. Similarly, maybe there are ways we are not providing the right environment for the seeds we have sown in someone else's life.

The only way we can provide this environment is to be an effective "Son-Sharer." Now, I can imagine some of you rolling your eyes at me. It sounds like corny wordsmithing a pastor might use in a sermon. And I get it…it kind of is, but it is also intentional.

I was going to use the term "sun-sharing" to describe this reality. But in the world of seeds we have been using as an illustration, there are many factors which help a seed germinate beyond just the sun and light, such as water, temperature, and oxygen. A seed can only germinate easily when all of these environmental factors are in the right proportion and balance.

More importantly, though, I use the term "son-sharing" because I wanted to remind us yet again that only the work of God that can bring about salvation. Hopefully, you have heard me be a broken record about this throughout the book. God is the One who does the work from beginning to end in the process of salvation and spiritual transformation. God not only designs the soil, seeds, and environment to work the way they do both naturally and spiritually, He is the One who sustains it.

Throughout this book we have also talked about the amazing message of the Kingdom of God: we have been invited to be co-workers with God. This means our role in producing the right environment in someone's life is not to control the environment completely. It is to share the Son, Jesus Christ, in various ways so that God can produce the right environment for the seeds to grow.

One of the big temptations that can arise for those of us who are in full time ministry is to become so enamored with trying to help people that we put the pressure on ourselves to save people. I have sat in many rooms with pastors and church leaders where the conversation is completely centered around things we can do to save people, or at least set the right environment. In those rooms, we desperately need to be reminded that only God can do that kind of work.

It would also be irresponsible for any of us to sit back and be lazy when God has called us to be co-workers in providing the right environment for the people around us. Think about 1 Peter 2:12. Peter says, "Live such good lives among the pagans that, though they accuse you of doing wrong, they may see your good deeds and glorify God on the day he visits us."[84] The call of Peter is to live in such a way to produce a right environment for those who might not be followers of Jesus yet.

Or ponder Matthew 5:13-16. In this passage from the Sermon on the Mount, Jesus gives two illustrations explaining who we are as followers of Jesus. The first, in Matthew 5:13 says, "You are the salt of the earth. But if the salt loses its saltiness, how can it be made salty again? It is no longer good for anything, except to be thrown out and trampled underfoot."[85] We, as people of God, are preserving agents bringing flavor and health to the environment. But if we fail to be who God has called us to be, we lose the potential of changing the environment.

The second illustration is that of light. In Matthew 5:14-16, Jesus says:

You are the light of the world. A town built on a hill cannot be hidden. Neither do people light a lamp and put it under a bowl. Instead they put it on its stand, and it gives light to everyone in the house. In the same way, let your light shine before others, that they may see your good deeds and glorify your father in heaven.[86]

We do not produce the saltiness or the light in us. God is the One who works in us to produce these things. And yet, He calls us to utilize them and share them with others. Jesus says it would be silly for people to light a lamp and then put it under a bowl. Light is meant to give guidance, direction, comfort, and clarity. When we live for God and intentionally share His Son with others through good deeds and right living, we can provide the correct environment for those seeds that were sown in others' lives to germinate.

When I consider the problems we face in being Son-Sharers, there are two opposite issues. The first is being too overbearing in our ministry to others. Sometimes, in our attempt to lead someone to Jesus we are overwhelming and intrusive. The opposite issue that can often affect the environment of someone's life is when we are too inconsistent. We want to sow seed and provide the right environment, but we are too inconsistent to produce any change in the environment of people's lives. If we are to find the proper way to share the Son with people around us, we must first take a look at how these polar opposite attitudes play out.

PROBLEM #1 – Too Overbearing

Do you ever people watch? I have to confess I am an avid people watcher. Not in a creepy way, but in a curious way. Especially when I am at a mall or large department store and wholly disinterested in the actual act of shopping, I tend to go into people watching mode. It is quite intriguing.

One of the most painful things for me to watch is how some parents interact with their children. You see all kinds of reactions. Parents yelling at kids in a demanding tone. Parents ignoring kids while they cry for what seems like an eternity. You can usually pick out helicopter parents as well.

These parents are always hovering over their kids, watching their every move. When someone talks to their child the parent is the one who answers back. They give their child clothes to try on while the child walks around like an obedient zombie. Any time some sort of life comes back into the child's face it is immediately snuffed out by their parents' controlling and overbearing words and actions.

Have you ever seen a parent like this? Are you a parent like this? For the most part, this overbearing parent is not trying to be detrimental to their child. They truly want what is best for them. But they also do not trust that their child's ideal life will come about without their constant intervention.

Sometimes you can literally see kids wilt before your very eyes due to the overbearing nature of their parents. The reason is because although kids need direction and shepherding, they wilt when they are cared for too much. It makes an environment by which the children do not know how to survive without their parents. In a similar way, out of a good heart, after we sow seed in people's lives we sometimes get overbearing in our Son-Sharing and ministry to those very people.

Being a pastor I hear many things about church life from different people. Over the years, one of the things I have heard from people who were just coming to faith or coming to church is how creepy the environment can be at first. They say people seem way too happy or welcoming.

Now, we hope as a church that we could be the most welcoming place in the entire world. And we believe that if someone is a follower of Jesus there should be a joy present in their life on a regular basis. So, I never fully grasped what they meant until I was on sabbatical last year.

Being that I work at a church, I do not get the opportunity to visit other churches very often. Therefore, I obviously do not get the opportunity to be a guest at a church very often. But on sabbatical I had four weeks that I attended church services at other places. They were all wonderful churches and they were not at all creepy. But at several of them I could understand how a person could feel overwhelmed. Out of a heart of wanting people to know Jesus and feel welcomed, the greeters or ushers or just regular church members were overbearing and over-welcoming. You tended to feel trapped by over-happy people that wanted something from you.

It was a good reminder to me about how in our ministry to others we must be careful to not be overbearing. I have watched many people over the years prepare soil well and sow seed well only to watch those seeds sown in someone's life begin to die. Like an overbearing parent, the person who has been trying to live a seed life starts to do everything for the person they are ministering to. They bring them to church and then start to control their interactions with people by talking for them instead of letting them talk for themselves. They start to over-spiritualize their interactions with the person and control all aspects of the environment of their heart. They push them to do and say spiritual things.

They have a good heart about it. They just want the person they are ministering to to understand it. The problem is that even if seed starts growing in someone's life, it is mainly manufactured and will not stand the real tests of life. It reminds me of what can often happen to plants that are sown indoors.

When you sow seeds inside you are putting them in a very controlled environment. People often buy trays from the store that have various little pods close together. They are perfectly spaced and small enough for one plant to grow per pod. If you wanted to sow seed in the pods you fill them with a special potting mix, put in some water, plant the seed, and then put them under a grow light.

A grow light is a special kind of light that produces particular wavelengths of the light spectrum that plants need to grow. You place these trays filled with soil and seed under the grow light and the waiting game begins. As the days and weeks go by, if conditions are right, those seeds germinate and start to grow into plants.

The problem comes when you try to take those plants you have had indoors, outside. You see, they have been raised in a completely controlled environment. They have not been forced to feel wind. They have not had to deal with temperature changes. They have not had to deal with changes in moisture levels. And most importantly, they have been growing by receiving artificial light.

If you were to take those plants outside and sow them directly into the soil, they would most likely die within days. Why? There could be a lot of reasons, but the primary reason is because you are taking a plant that was used to artificial light and exposing it to the great and awesome power of the sun.

Now let's put this in spiritual terms. When we minister to people in an overbearing way or when churches set up their ministry to people in an overbearing way, we are trying to control all aspects of the environment of their lives. Instead of trusting the Holy Spirit to guide that person in their faith and us only intervening to the level of sharing the Son with that person, we feel like we have to control every aspect of their life.

The focus is often on programs, principles, and practices. Church ministries that act this way focus all of their attention on getting people to feel good and be comfortable. Instead of real and authentic relationships they put people in programs so that things can be efficient. Instead of helping someone to learn to read the Bible and pray, they focus on watered-down principles they say are easier for people. The end result, whether intentional or not, is to be a good person who serves other people and gets "involved."

Now, I am not saying all programs, principles, and practices are wrong. But focusing on programs, principles, and practices apart from the Gospel, the presence of God, the Bible, prayer, and authentic relationships is like sowing seeds indoors. It is artificial. You are trying to grow something through human means. And something produced through human means will never survive in the real world. It reminds me of what is said in Isaiah 29:13: "The Lord says: 'These people come near to me with their mouth and honor me with their lips, but their hearts are far from me. Their worship of me is based on merely human rules they have been taught.'"[87]

I cannot tell you how many parents I talked to when I was a college pastor who told me the same story. They talked about their child, whom they loved dearly, who was raised in the church but now wanted nothing to do with faith. They thought they had done everything right. They felt as though they had their child in the right programs, learning the right principles and teaching their kids what they considered to be good practices. They talked about how their child who was now a college student was a kind and good person who was highly involved in the things they are passionate about. And yet, there was nothing they could do to get them interested in faith. The child hit the "real world" and the seeds their parents thought they sowed in them did not survive the process of taking them outside.

It always broke my heart. The parents of these college students would be pleading for me to do something for them and I would gladly try. But the process would have to start all over again with sowing the seeds of the Gospel in them. And this time it could not happen artificially. Prayer and the work of the Holy Spirit was going to be the primary way these students would come to Jesus.

PROBLEM #2 – Too Inconsistent

On the opposite side of being too overbearing is being too inconsistent. You can often see this in the lives of people who are too busy. Too busy with work, hobbies, family, ministry, or something else. Many of them have great intentions. They want to have it all. And many of them do have a heart to see people come to know Jesus. In fact, many of them may be participating in ministries or ministry programs where they are trying to be soil-builders and seed-sowers. But they are not being effective Son-sharers and providing a good environment for those seeds to grow in.

In order for seeds to germinate well, one of the factors that must be right is moisture. The soil must be moist, but not too soggy. One of the things seeds and seedlings do not like is inconsistent moisture. When plants are full-grown it is easier for them to deal with some inconsistencies in watering, but when seeds are just germinating moisture must be consistent.

One of the ways to make sure you have constant moisture levels is to have drip irrigation. Drip irrigation comes from hoses that spread out around your garden area with holes near each one of your seedlings. When you turn on the water, it drips water at those spots in order to keep moisture levels consistent. It provides a little bit of moisture all the time instead of a lot of water all at once.

Bucket irrigation is the opposite. Bucket irrigation means you wait until things dry out and then you pour a bucket full of water over the seedlings. When plants are older this can be an effective form of watering because it helps the plant develop deeper roots. But for a seedling this can mean instant death. Pouring too much water on a seedling can make the soil soggy and choke out the roots, or even wash seeds away. Seeds and seedlings would rather have a little bit of moisture all the time instead of a lot of water all at once.

In a similar way, when we are inconsistent with people we have been sowing seeds into, we can be like that bucket irrigation. There are so many blessings to being one of the pastors at a large church like ours, but there are also some downsides. One of the downsides is that unless we are really careful, people can fall through the cracks. My spiritual formation team oversees thirty to fifty different small groups depending on the time of the year. We also oversee a volunteer counseling ministry that meets with several people each week. We also oversee the initial steps people can take in knowing Jesus and joining the church. Depending on the time of the year there could be as many as four hundred people who are involved in ministries we oversee and these people can be all over the spectrum of spiritual growth.

Now, I am not the one who is supposed to be directly ministering to each of these people. I am to equip lay leaders to be the hands and feet of Jesus. But I do have a responsibility to keep an eye on people, especially those who may not be Christians yet or are just coming into a relationship with Jesus. My heart breaks most when someone who is on the fringe of knowing Jesus walks away. Sometimes this has nothing to do with us, but other times I am convicted of the fact we had inconsistent ministry to them. We were like those who brought the bucket of grace over and unloaded a bunch of information and help on a person, but then were absent when they had questions or were struggling.

Maybe you have seen this in your own life. You may not oversee a specific ministry, but you are ministering to the circle of influence you have been given. You get excited because you got the chance to talk to one of your co-workers about Jesus. You have been preparing the soil and sowing seeds in their life for a while and now you got the chance to share about a relationship with Jesus. But after this amazing conversation, you got busy at work and at home and forgot to even think about that conversation.

When you finally remember having that conversation a couple weeks or months later, you might try continuing the conversation with your co-worker but there seems to be a barrier now. The person has their defenses up because when there is inconsistent ministry people can start to feel like a project. They feel as though you are in it for yourself instead of actually caring about them. It feels to them like they are simply a notch on your belt of goodness or another task to be accomplished instead of a person you truly care about.

We have to be careful not to be overbearing in our ministry to others but also not too inconsistent. So how do we help produce the right environment in the people around us without going to the extremes?

HOW SHOULD WE HELP?

When I think of healthy Son-Sharing the picture of a hoop house comes to mind. A hoop house is an unheated greenhouse of sorts. Basically, it is a shell made from wood, cattle fence panels, or PVC pipe that is put over a patch of soil and covered with greenhouse plastic. The concept of a hoop house is pretty simple. The plastic protects the seeds and seedlings that are growing within from the worst of the weather while also amplifying the heat of the sun to help the seeds grow.

Now, because it is unheated it still can get cold in a hoop house. But at least on days when it is sunny the hoop house amplifies the sun's warmth to make conditions right for seeds to grow. This means I can start certain plants in our garden outside in March or April. There could be snow on the ground outside but those seeds can still germinate if the sun is shining. It can be thirty degrees outside but if it is a sunny day it could be in the sixties in the hoop house.

The nice thing about a hoop house is you can sow seeds directly outside instead of inside. And since they get used to the temperatures and sunlight and other elements of being outdoors you do not have to worry about them surviving or not. When things warm up in late spring you simply take off the plastic and you are left with a beautiful garden.

What if we started to see ourselves more as hoop houses than people who sow seeds indoors? Hoop houses do not completely control the environment or even necessarily remove the soil and seed from the harsh and wild environment of outside. Instead, they help to provide the right environment by covering the soil and seed. They cover the soil in order to amplify the sun. In a similar way, what if we saw our primary job as amplifying and sharing the Son in the lives of people around us?

Prayer

One way of doing this is through prayer. I hope you have noticed the importance of prayer throughout this book. As you may have realized in the application sections throughout the book, prayer is almost always included. The reason is because God is the One who is going to produce spiritual work in someone's life. So the best thing we could possibly do is to pray for Him to work. In this case, think of prayer as the greenhouse plastic of a hoop house. It is an amplifier of God's presence.

In John 8:12 it says, "When Jesus spoke again to the people, he said, "I am the light of the world. Whoever follows me will never walk in darkness, but will have the light of life."[88] Earlier in John it says this about Jesus, "In him was life, and that life was the light of all mankind. The light shines in the darkness, and the darkness has not overcome it."[89] Jesus, the Son of God, is the light that brings life. He is the One who brings dead things to life and the One who brings dark things into the light. He is the One who thaws out the frozen heart.

And His light is always shining. God wants all mankind to know Him. In fact, 1 Timothy 2:3-4 says, "This is good, and pleases God our savior, who wants all people to be saved and to come to a knowledge of the truth."[90] But in the midst of the frozen spiritual tundra of this world, people still cannot feel the light of God shining on them because the soil and seeds are not in the right environment to bring forth life.

When we pray, it is like covering the soil and amplifying the sun's rays to shine on those seeds that have been planted. We are commanded to pray in Matthew 6:10, "Your kingdom come, your will be done, on earth as it is in heaven."[91] When we intercede for someone else, we are asking God's kingdom to come in their lives. We are asking for those seeds of the Gospel to awaken.

When Janelle and I were going to have our first child, Judah, we were given a book called, "60 Promises to Pray Over Your Children," by Roy Lessin. When she was pregnant we would look at that book every night and pray one of the pages over our son. There were different types of prayer: prayers of blessing, protection, growth, character, and many others. Even after he was born, but before he could understand us, I would place my hand on his head and pray those prayers over him.

Someone might ask, "Why did you do that when he couldn't even understand what you were praying over him?" The prayers were not for him directly, they were for God. They were pleadings for God to work in Judah's life. We wanted to "raise the temperature" in Judah's life so that the seeds we were sowing in his life would come to fruition.

So the first, and primary way, we can be a Son-Sharer in the lives of people around us is to be praying for the temperature to rise in the environment of their lives.

Presence

Another way to be a Son-Sharer in the lives of people around us is to provide presence. Another benefit of the greenhouse plastic on a hoop house is that it helps to retain moisture. If you go inside a hoop house after a sunny day you will see moisture beaded up all over the inside of the plastic. If you accidentally bump the hoop house all that water comes down on your head (which is not fun).

The point is, one of the problems we talked about is inconsistency in ministry. When we provide presence in someone's life it can help retain the right moisture level for seeds to grow. Being present is allowing the love of Jesus, the Living Water, to be present in that person's life until the seeds of the Gospel germinate in them as well.

In John 4, Jesus is talking to a Samaritan woman at a well. Jews and Samaritans did not normally get along and women and men did not normally talk so openly in the society of that day, but Jesus crossed over those kinds of lines all the time to show His love to people. As He talks to her, He says in John 4:10, "If you knew the gift of God and who it is that asks you for a drink, you would have asked him and he would have given you living water."[92]

A couple verses later He says, "Everyone who drinks this water will be thirsty again, but whoever drinks the water I give them will never thirst. Indeed, the water I give them will become in them a spring of water welling up to eternal life."[93] Jesus is the Living Water that awakens seeds to life. What He demonstrated with the woman at the well, other than just explaining about Living Water is that He is a God of presence. He comes near to those who need Him.

When we provide consistent presence in someone's life we are allowing space for the Living Water to do His work. We are present with time, resources, love, attention, and a listening ear. We are intentional to be around that person consistently. We are intentional to use our resources to bless them, not just once but consistently. When we are with them we are not distracted but present. We spend time with them even if a spiritual conversation does not arise or if there is not "progress." We are just there.

We listen and only speak when we believe God wants them to hear something. We give our time and resources not expecting something in return but because we love them. We encourage them, we pray for them when they are willing, we invite them deeper. We are not afraid to ask and push the conversation about Jesus forward in their life but we also have a sensitivity to stop when they wish to stop. If there is resistance in their hearts, we pray and stay present until God breaks down that wall of resistance. We are relentless with invitation but not overbearing through control.

This covering of presence allows people to consistently have the Spirit of God at work around them. We are temples of the Holy Spirit according 1 Corinthians 6:19. Where we go, the Spirit of God goes with us. An environment saturated with the presence of God is ripe for seeds to start to germinate.

This is why I love to think about partnering with others in Son-Sharing. One of the first things I do with people I am ministering to is introduce them to other people around me who are passionate about Jesus. This may mean introducing them to my wife or one of my ministry teammates or lay leaders in the ministries I oversee. When I do this and can partner in ministry with others, it saturates the environment of that person's life more and more with Son-Sharers.

Each one of us can share aspects of presence with that person. I know that my wife can bless someone with generosity a hundred times better than I can. She knows exactly how to encourage people with beautiful cards, notes, cookies, and many other things. I am terrible at this. But the presence I can often bring in someone's life that might be harder for her are intentional spiritual questions. When we partner together we bring different aspects of the love of God to bear.

Protection

One other way we can be Son-Sharers and provide a good environment for seeds to grow is to provide protection. We have an enemy who stands against us, Satan. He does not want those seeds that have been planted in peoples' lives to come to fruition. Every person who has the Seed of Life germinate in them and become a wonderfully productive disciple in the Kingdom of God is a threat and abomination to him. He would want nothing more than to "steal and kill and destroy" those seeds so that people could never come to a saving knowledge of Jesus Christ.[94]

In fact, in Mark 4 where Jesus tells the parable of the sower that we looked at earlier in the book, Satan's actions are explained. Jesus gives the picture of a farmer out sowing seed. He explains that some of it "fell along the path, and the birds came and ate it up."[95] Later on in the chapter He explains the meaning of this to the disciples. He says in Mark 4:14-15, "The farmer sows the word. Some people are like seed along the path, where the word is sown. As soon as they hear it, Satan comes and takes away the word that was sown in them."[96] What we can take from this is that Satan wants to distract, tempt, or take away any hope of a person coming into a saving relationship with Jesus.

If that is the case, one of the most important ways we can provide the right environment for seeds to grow in someone's life is to provide protection. Another way the plastic on a hoop house is helpful is that it provides protection. Other than creatures that can bury underground and get into the soil that way, the seeds that are sown are protected from birds or deer or any creature that might want to disturb the soil and seeds.

In a similar way, when we choose to surround someone with protection, we are leaving less room for the enemy to attack. So how does this look? Recently I was reading 1 John 4:4 where it says, "You, dear children, are from God and have overcome them, because the one who is in you is greater than the one who is in the world."[97] We carry inside of us the One who is greater than any attack the enemy can bring. We carry the "mind of Christ" within us.[98] The weapons we fight with have "divine power to demolish strongholds."[99]

Therefore, when we are ministering to someone who is open to the Gospel but has not accepted it yet, we keep a watchful eye over them. If anyone tries to convince them of something that is not of God, we offer the true Word of God. When unbelieving friends around them start to pull them down and tear them away from pursuing God, we offer true friendship. When there is a wrestling in their spirit over what to believe, we fast and pray for them. We do whatever it takes to provide protection as God works life into them.

Several years ago I was working with someone who had recently come to our church. They had serious emotional wounds and also were living out a lifestyle that was completely against the ways of God. I provided prayer, guidance, and presence. There were several of us pastors ministering to this person. You could tell that God was doing some incredible things to provide the right environment in their heart.

I began to do prayer counseling sessions with this person and things were going well. Then I could sense some deep resistance to moving forward and being transformed by God. As I probed a little deeper into what this resistance was I found out it was a sense of obligation to a group of friends this person had. The group of friends was severely opposed to this person following the ways of God. You could sense the spiritual struggle.

I realized that although I and others had provided prayer and presence, we must also offer up protection. I fought and fought on their behalf providing time, resources, counsel, and prayer. We had several intense prayer counseling sessions, but despite all of this, the person still walked away. Sometimes that will happen; we cannot control peoples' actions. Yet, we tried our best to be Son-Sharers. I still think about this person and am praying they will come back at some point.

I could tell you story after story of people who seemed to be on the edge and I needed to help provide protection for them. God was gracious and many of those people are thriving in their relationship with Jesus today. In fact, several of them are involved in some sort of ministry now. But whether people respond to it or not, we must provide protection for those we have planted seeds into.

CONCLUSION

So what kind of environment are you providing in the lives of people around you? Are you overbearing? If so, I am not telling you to completely give up and not do anything. I am simply asking you to trust God and listen to Him as you minister to people. If you try to control every aspect of your ministry to someone, you are at best contributing to them becoming a consumer Christian and at worst you are misrepresenting the Gospel.

Trust God. He loves them more than you can possibly imagine. If you think you love them, your love is like a drop in a bucket compared to how much He loves them, and He wants what is best for them. Just listen to God and minister to them as they are ready.

Are you too inconsistent in your ministry to others? Does your busyness or apathy lead you down a path of unintentionally making people feel like they are projects? Then ask yourself what your true mission is in this world; what will really matter after this life is over? All that will matter is how many people we have invested in and shared the love of God with. This is our life if we are followers of Jesus. Pray for a sensitivity to the needs of people around you. Pray for God to give you a consistent and overwhelming sense of love for people who need to know Him.

And as you go, be a Son-Sharer by providing temperature-raising prayer, Living Water-inspired presence, and divinely enabled protection so those seeds that have been sown in someone's life may germinate into a wonderful relationship with Jesus Christ!

REFLECTION QUESTIONS

1. The chapter began by talking about the word "environment." We can prepare soil, sow seeds, and still the environment of someone's life may not allow that spiritual seed to grow. Do you have an example of someone in your life who is like this? You have prepared their heart, sown seeds, and yet they still do not receive the Gospel?

2. The word "Son-sharing" was used to describe providing the right environment in someone's life after seeds have been sown. In nature these environmental factors might

be sun, moisture, air, etc. What are some examples of environmental factors in a spiritual sense?

3. One of the ways we miss out on providing the right environment in someone's life is when we are overbearing in our ministry to them. On a scale of 1-10, how would you rate how overbearing you are in relationships with others? How might this affect your ministry to someone you are trying to share the Gospel with?

4. Another way we may miss out on providing the right environment in someone's life is when we are too inconsistent in our ministry to them. On a scale of 1-10, how would you rate how inconsistent you are in relationships to others? How might this affect your ministry to someone you are trying to share the Gospel with?

5. Did anything else stand out to you from this chapter?

APPLICATION

1. PRAYER – We have talked about prayer several times throughout this book. If you have not already started praying more regularly for people in your life to come to salvation, here is another reminder to start. Also, consider inviting others to come alongside you in prayer for people.

2. PRESENCE – How can you be more present with someone this week that you have lost sight of? Maybe it means getting together for coffee, texting them every day, setting up a game night, or something else.

3. PROTECTION – Ask the Lord to give you a watchful eye over those you are ministering to. Pray for protection over them from Satan and ask the Lord for wisdom if you need to intervene in some way.

Seed Life Spotlight
STORIES OF OVERFLOW
By Sherrill Auker

"We're growing old. We're about to leave this place, but you have more time: practice this and pass it on to others." Eighty-five-year-old Philip stood before the community group, urging others to join the mission. His life had been transformed near its end - now he prays his children and younger neighbors will understand sooner. The Lord proved Himself Provider to Philip, faithfully establishing the work of Philip's hands as he returned his field to its real Owner. As he shared his testimony, he laughed, "I kept asking: Why do these people pray for me after they visit my field every time? Finally I realized that everything I have - even my strength - I owe to God."

Philip spends his days actively practicing Farming God's Way and teaching others. The Lord has so greatly changed his life that he cannot remain quiet. This is the simplicity of evangelism. Evangelism is a recognition of who God is, an overflow from a grateful life. It says, "Look at how great God is! Look at what He's done! He can do the same for you!"

Such is the confidence and steadfast reliance and absolute trust that we have through Christ toward God. Not that we are sufficiently qualified in ourselves to claim anything as coming from us, but our sufficiency and qualifications come from God. He has qualified us (making us sufficient) as ministers of a new covenant…[100]

An eighty-five-year-old, new minister doesn't base decisions on educational background, societal perception, or family opinions. Only one line item resides on his list of qualifications: Jesus. He walks daily with a confidence that Christ is His sufficiency.

Our living with this mindset transforms each moment into an opportunity for evangelism. Realizing Christ is our qualifier throws off the weight of saying the perfect words or setting up a textbook altar call. Instead, we can walk in the freedom of the Spirit, unhindered by the concerns that focus our attention on us. We are ministers, seeing any connection point with people as an opportunity.

Ministry is simply living with an awareness that God wants to work through you. As carriers of the Holy Spirit, we can change the atmosphere of any setting. God Himself has chosen to take up residence in us, not a lofty conscience or inner GPS. The very Spirit of the living, powerful God decided His home was in His people. We can live with incredible expectation. Every interaction can be filled with His grace, can communicate His openness and kindness. With each step, we can create an environment that conveys *there's more to this life*, a paradox uniting conviction and welcome.

But even in our absence, the Spirit is moving, cultivating the land where seed has been sown. We do not stuff God in a backpack and let him out, introducing Him to neighbors and friends. He's present, always working, even when we are unaware. As we consistently change the atmosphere, walking with a willingness to serve, He'll even bring those who are searching to your very doorstep.

The popcorn balanced on the small propane stove. An impromptu team party broke out after an exciting meeting. Pastors from 11 denominations had gathered in one home, believing for a different future for the Democratic Republic of Congo. Years ago, these individuals were enemies, angry to even sit in the same room. Today, they minister together, meet for prayer, and unify their community. A beautiful commissioning prayer brought us all into agreement: DRC will be known for peace, becoming a sanctuary. The Lord is giving this nation a new name.

Though the hour was late, our small team broke out snacks and card games, too ecstatic to turn in for the night. Gaston wandered outside for a phone call, a common action for the busy lawyer.

Soon, he popped his head back inside, "Someone is here to see us. Can we meet with them?" We quickly cleaned up the room and a mother, son, and daughter entered. The daughter had a severe rash and coughing. The mother was in extreme stomach pain. We gathered around Marie, the daughter, first, and invited her mother Beatrice to lead us in prayer. She placed a hand on the struggling young girl, and we joined in prayer. Then Beatrice kneeled to the ground.

She soon lifted her head, a flood of relief over her face. She sighed "Merci!" with gentleness and joy after touching her stomach quickly in surprise. I spoke up: "You've shown great faith, and God is even going to increase it."

Gaston laughed, confirming my words, "It's true! They were trying to turn her away outside and have her come back tomorrow. She and her family were getting back from the hospital, where the doctors couldn't tell them what the problem was. She thought that sometimes people get prayed for at this house and persisted."

The following morning as we packed our tents, Beatrice arrived to fetch water and visit us. Her daughter's rash was clearing up, and the Lord had continued His conversation with her. Beatrice met Him in her desperation but remains in His faithful love.

Ministry is in the interruptions, hidden in the occasions where *later* could be a reasonable response. Attentiveness is crucial. When we are consumed with our own agenda, we create an environment of hurriedness, bringing distance between us and others. We miss the quiet voices, the broken hearts, the compounding needs lingering in the background. Instead, we can resolve to live slower with an openness to His leading, purposefully present to the people who surround us. Jesus mastered the life of interruptions even when others tried to push him into the regular stream of activity.

In Mark 10, Bartimaeus, a blind man, sat by the roadside as Jesus and a large crowd left Jericho. When Bartimaeus identified Jesus, he immediately shouted, "Jesus, Son of David, have mercy on me!"[101] He knew the stories. He had confidence in Jesus' miraculous life. Those nearby attempted to silence him, as if protecting Jesus from one more beggar. But the blind man only increased his volume, undeterred by the opinions of the fortunate. Jesus, constantly walking with an awareness of the needs surrounding him, stopped.

"Call him."

Those that once shushed him, now changed their language. "Take heart. Get up; he is calling you."[102] Bartimaeus immediately jumped up and ran. Jesus asked him a simple question: "What do you want me to do for you?"[103]

The blind man requests a miracle. Jesus delivers one. Recovered sight results in a new heart. A dedicated follower was born that day.

"What do you want me to do for you?" Jesus' question echoes today. We know His promises; we're familiar with His abilities. But what are we actually expecting? We ask Jesus to bless our food, to help us have a good day, to save us a close parking spot.

We settle for so small an ask, when He longs to give us the nations.

> *Arise, shine, for your light has come,*
> *and the glory of the Lord has risen upon you.*
> *For behold, darkness shall cover the earth,*
> *and thick darkness the peoples;*
> *but the Lord will arise upon you,*
> *and his glory will be seen upon you.*
> *And nations shall come to your light,*
> *and kings to the brightness of your rising.*[104]

The only limitations are the ones we place on ourselves. The promises of God are beyond our imagination; His desire to use us far exceeds our understanding. Our requirements: Go and speak. Live mindful to His heart for those around you.

The Samaritan woman ran out with a simple testimony, only a glimpse of the story. Yet, an entire village soon walked to the well, discovering the Living Water themselves.

We've seen the lame walk, the oppressed freed, the sick healed. We've walked through relationship reconciliation, land restoration, and promises realized. Alcoholism has been broken; anxiety has fled, and the lost have returned to their Father.

Let us be the ones willing to believe for more. The ones embodying a full recognition of identity in Christ, a deep understanding of His heart for people. We can carry the atmosphere of freedom, leaving the *Kingdom of God* on every footprint in our wake.

Until our friends, communities, and the whole world hear—we GO.

7

Seed Life Training Plan
TRANSLATING LEARNING INTO ACTION

I was walking my dog along a dirt road the other day and I was struck by the dichotomy of the situation. On one hand, it was a beautiful walk. The quiet was palpable, the faint babbling brook and trees blowing in the wind being the only noises keeping it from complete silence. The trees creaked and groaned as soldiers of winter, standing stripped of their glorious summer garb. The winding road seemed to lead further and further up and around as I walked.

This dirt road is a great place to think and pray. However, my thinking and praying was being disrupted by our crazy dog. We have an eight-month old Vizsla puppy that we were given this past summer. We struggled through whether to accept him or not because we had our second child in September.

We knew it already would be an eventful year, but I knew when I married my wife I would have to get a dog at some point. She was a Veterinary Technician for a long time. She has always loved animals. I, on the other hand, never had a pet because I was allergic to most animals. I was not used to having a dog, but I knew it was only a matter of time before it happened.

I had wanted to wait until our oldest child was old enough to appreciate having a dog and he was starting to get to that age. Then, the opportunity to get a free Vizsla came along. This was the kind of dog my wife always wanted and they are typically quite expensive. Despite the knowledge that we were having a baby in a couple of months, we decided to go ahead and get the puppy. We named him Jett.

Jett is a fun dog, but Vizslas are by nature very energetic dogs. With the baby being born and life happening we have not had as much time as we hoped to train him. We are working on it but the dog is not quite there yet.

So as I am taking this walk through the peaceful woods, I fluctuate between times of great peace and tranquility and my crazy dog trying to drag me into the woods. I give him the commands to sit and heel and we start walking again. Then, all of sudden, he goes into hyper mode again.

As I thought about our dog and his resistance to being trained, I contemplated what we should do with what we've learned from the parables of Jesus about the Kingdom of God. Throughout *Seed Life* the encouragement has been to reorient our mindsets about evangelism around the Kingdom of God.

When we do this, amazing things can happen. Just like a disrupted and overgrown garden can be brought back into order and fruitfulness, so God wants to bring this dark and broken world back into beauty. His plan of doing this involves making each one of us fruitful so our lives can multiply the Seed of the Gospel into others.

One of the main points I have been trying to make is that if we are pursuing Jesus in our lives, then engaging every person with a Kingdom mindset is a natural byproduct. Or a better way of saying it is that it is a supernatural process, but it occurs naturally in us as we get closer and closer to God.

But just as our dog resists training even in the midst of such a beautiful walk, so our souls resist the fruitfulness God wants for us. Although evangelism should be a naturally supernatural response to our recognition of the Kingdom of God, we must train our souls to continue to engage every person with a Kingdom mindset.

I have not met a single Christian who would say they are not interested in other people coming to know Jesus. Yet, if you were to ask them how their own mission is going with reaching people for Jesus, they would bashfully talk about a quick conversation they had with a neighbor or a program they are involved with. Deep down they know their life is not as fruitful as it should be.

They know their soul is being distracted by all sorts of things: busyness, their own comfort, anxiety, etc. There may be moments of fruitfulness followed by their soul running away from that fruitfulness. It may be easy for them to engage some people with a Kingdom mindset, but it feels impossible to engage every person with a Kingdom mindset.

So how do we train our souls? If we take a look at how we train our dog, it means continually putting the dog into situations where he needs training. Then, in the midst of that situation, we keep reorienting his attention back to our commands.

In order to train our souls, we must continually put our souls into situations that would force us to engage people with a Kingdom mindset. And, in the midst of those situations, we must orient our souls to the commands of God.

Below is a tentative plan to shift your life from what it is currently into a productive Seed Life. Now, a plan in and of itself will do nothing for you, but if you view this plan as a way to train your soul it may help to guide your efforts in living a *Seed Life*. Please take time to pray and reflect on each segment as you write down your Seed Life training plan.

SEED LIFE TRAINING PLAN

EVALUATE

*Identify three key thoughts from the book that most challenged you:

*Identify three suggested action steps in the book that made you most uncomfortable:

*Based on the previous two lists, write down where you believe God wants to make you more effective in having a Seed Life:

PLAN

*God wants to make me more fruitful in my Seed Life by:

*If I am to grow in this area I need to put myself in a position to be stretched by taking these steps:

1.

2.

3.

*As I take these three steps, I will remember God's commands by:

*I will invite _____ into this process, asking them to be an accountability partner or challenging them to join me in taking these steps.

*As I see God work in these steps I will pass the story onto others by:

OTHER KEY ESSENTIALS TO A SEED LIFE

*If you have never done the things below, consider investing energy into them:

A PRAYER JOURNAL – Keep a journal specifically to pray for people who have not started a relationship with God yet.

WRITE OUT YOUR TESTIMONY – Take some time to write out your testimony on a single sheet of paper. Getting your testimony down concisely on one sheet of paper helps you have clarity if someone asks about it.

HAVE A CLEAR UNDERSTANDING OF HOW TO SHARE THE GOSPEL – Study a new way of sharing the Gospel. *ENGAGE: How to Know God* has a clear process for sharing the Gospel, or you could memorize the "Romans Road." There are many other ways of sharing the Gospel. Consult a pastor or trusted Christian friend about ways they have chosen to share the Good News.

CONCLUSION

As I sit here finishing this book, it is the day before my wife's grandmother's funeral. She was a wonderful woman who was 93 years old. I had known her since I started dating my wife, which has been almost a decade. She was kind and sweet, with a gentle demeanor. Grammy was always trying to deflect attention away from herself back to God and others. She had a large legacy, with a family line down to great-great-grandkids. I am honored to have known her.

As the family was beginning to clean out the house, they came across a notebook Grammy had written in. There were various notes about the grass being cut, the weather that day, and other mundane things. Then, there were profound quotes written on other pages. Most of them did not have any acknowledgement, so we are not sure whether these quotes were ones she heard or something she came up with herself.

One page simply had this scribbled on it:

Never give up on anyone's salvation. You may not live to see the fruit, but plant all the Gospel seeds you can.

What a powerful statement! Whether it was a quote of her own or something she had heard, I think it is a fitting way to end this journey of learning about a seed life.

Throughout this book, I have tried to persuade you that your fears about sharing the Gospel with other people are unfounded, because they are based on a misconception of what evangelism actually means.

We looked at parables in the gospels where Jesus compares the Kingdom of God to a garden. He is the seed that was planted to redeem the "corrupted garden" of fallen humanity. He is searching for good soil, where He can plant His seed of life and produce transformation in the lives of you and me. As we simply let Him do His work and grow into the plant He wants us to be, He allows us to become co-workers with Him in His mission to redeem the world. When we intentionally engage every person with a Kingdom mindset He uses us to become soil-building, seed-sowing, Son-sharing members of the Kingdom of God.

We no longer *do* evangelism; we *are* evangelists because we engage every person with a Kingdom mindset. We no longer just set aside time to do evangelistic projects; every word we speak and every act we do is an opportunity to prepare soil, sow seeds, or share Jesus with someone. We no longer think that only "professional" Christians can share the Gospel with others; we realize that we all have a part to play. We no longer fear evangelism; we realize it is our great joy and honor to be representatives of Jesus Christ to the world.

We have explored a whole new way of looking at evangelism, but we have yet to talk about the word most associated with evangelism: harvest. Pastors, evangelists, and missionaries use the word "harvest" when they are hosting a revival or evangelistic event. The "harvest" describes people who actually start a relationship with Jesus. And it makes sense why this is our hope. You do not prepare soil and plant a seed without expecting a harvest.

The harvest picture is used in the Bible quite often. In Luke 10:2 Jesus says, "The harvest is plentiful, but the workers are few. Ask the Lord of the harvest, therefore, to send out workers into his harvest field."[105] Paul in Romans 1:13 talks about His hope in coming to the Romans being "that I might have a harvest among you."[106]

We should be yearning for a harvest! My prayer is that each person reading this book would get to participate in many, many harvests of souls for the Kingdom throughout their lifetime. We must be willing to ask people whether they want to start a relationship with Jesus when the time is right. We must know how to share our testimony and how to share the Gospel clearly with those who are ready to hear it. I commend you to learn how to do these things if you do not know yet. I wrote the book *ENGAGE: How to Know God* for the very purpose of teaching people what the Gospel is and how to share it with others. There are also many other resources out there or people in your church who would be more than happy to help teach you how to do these things.

However, despite how important it is to learn these things, we too often gauge our success in evangelism on whether a harvest has happened or not. I have had the privilege of leading people into a relationship with Jesus over my lifetime. I have also faithfully ministered to many people for years without them coming to know Jesus until they went somewhere else or heard someone else share the Gospel with them.

I did not gauge my interest in investing in their life on whether they were going to lead to a harvest. I, like all of us, have been called to live a seed life. And if we are called to live out a seed life, harvests may come quickly or they may not. Harvests may never come at all in your lifetime. But as Grammy's notebook said, *"Never give up on anyone's salvation. You may not live to see the fruit, but plant all the Gospel seeds you can."*

I promise you: if every single one of us was living a seed life, there would be no need to worry about a lack of harvest. Everywhere we look there would be seeds that were sown coming to life and producing fruit. If we were to be honest with ourselves, however, so few of us are being soil-builders, seed-sowers, and Son-sharers on a continual basis. Living a seed life is not glamorous. It takes all that we are as we surrender to God's will and God's way. It takes cultivation and patience.

In Galatians 6:9 it says, "Let us not become weary in doing good, for at the proper time we will reap a harvest if we do not give up."[107] I think this is a great encouragement for us. We do not need to worry about the harvest. We will reap a harvest at the proper time, when God ordains it. But whether there is a harvest in the short term or no harvest at all, we must faithfully keep living out a seed life.

It is our one great calling in this life.

When I think about Grammy's funeral, I know countless people will be in attendance who have been touched by her life. She was not flashy. She did not get up in front of large crowds. She would not have considered herself a Bible scholar. But she was faithful to live out the calling of God on her life. She lived a seed life. I can think of no more fitting way to finish this book than to encourage you one more time to take Grammy's advice:

Never give up on anyone's salvation.
You may not live to see the fruit, but plant all the Gospel seeds you can.

[1] Mark Synott, "Exclusive: Alex Honnold Completes the Most Dangerous Free-Solo Ascent Ever," *National Geographic*, National Geographic Partners, LLC, 3 Oct. 2018, www.nationalgeographic.com/adventure/features/athletes/alex-honnold/most-dangerous-free-solo-climb-yosemite-national-park-el-capitan/.

[2] Genesis 2:8 and 2:15 NIV

[3] "Farm Population Lowest Since 1850's." *The New York Times*, The New York Times Company, 20 July 1988, www.nytimes.com/1988/07/20/us/farm-population-lowest-since-1850-s.html.

[4] Joel Salatin, *The Marvelous Pigness of Pigs: Respecting and Caring for All God's Creation* (New York, NY: Faithwords, 2017), p. 13.

[5] R.T. France, "Matthew: An Introduction and Commentary," in *Tyndale Commentary*, ed. Leon Morris (Illinois: Intervarsity Press, 1987), 49.

[6] 1 Cor. 13:1-3 NIV

[7] Romans 7:5 NIV

[8] Genesis 2:16-17 NIV

[9] Matthew 13:24b-26, NIV

[10] Matthew 13:30 NIV

[11] Matthew 13:37-39 NIV

[12] Matthew 13:41b NIV

[13] John 12:23-24 NIV

[14] Romans 5:8 NIV

[15] Joel Salatin, *The Marvelous Pigness of Pigs: Respecting and Caring for All God's Creation* (New York, NY: Faithwords,

2017), p. 48.

[16] John 15:1 NIV

[17] John 12:24 NIV

[18] 1 Corinthians 3:5-9 NIV

[19] 1 Corinthians 3:9 NIV

[20] Revelation 1:6 NIV

[21] Matthew 6:10 NIV

[22] Isaiah 62:6 ESV

[23] Matthew 28:19 ESV

[24] John 14:12 ESV

[25] Matthew 7:7 ESV

[26] Acts 4:13 ESV

[27] Acts 6:2 ESV

[28] Acts 6:8 ESV

[29] 2 Corinthians 5:17-19

[30] Romans 6:4 ESV

[31] Romans 6:11 ESV

[32] Dana Richardson and Sarah Zentz, directors. *Back to Eden*. Dana and Sarah Films, 2011.

[33] Mark 4:3-8 NIV

[34] Mark 4:14-20 NIV

[35] English, Donald, "The Message of Mark," in *The Bible Speaks Today*, ed. John R.W. Stott (Illinois: Intervaristy Press, 1995), 94.

[36] English, Donald, "The Message of Mark," in *The Bible Speaks Today*, 94.

[37] "Till," Dictionary.com, accessed November 13, 2018, https://www.dictionary.com/browse/till.

[38] Hosea 10:12-13a NIV

[39] Hosea 10:12 NIV

[40] 2 Peter 3:18 NIV

[41] 1 Corinthians 8:1 NIV

[42] Joel Salatin, *The Marvelous Pigness of Pigs: Respecting and Caring for All God's Creation* (New York, NY: Faithwords, 2017), p. 51.

[43] "Compost," Dictionary.com, accessed November 13, 2018, https://www.dictionary.com/browse/compost.

[44] Ecclesiastes 3:11 NIV

[45] John 6:44 NIV

[46] John 6:65 NIV

[47] John 15:1-2 NIV

[48] 1 Peter 3:1-2 NIV

[49] Philippians 2:5-8 NIV

[50] Tom Price, "Starting With Questions" *Pulse*, Issue 8 (Summer 2011), pp. 12-13.

[51] Zacharias, Ravi. "Four Components of a Worldview." *Just a Thought Podcast*, RZIM, 25 July 2018, www.rzim.org/listen/just-a-thought/four-components-of-a-worldview-jat

[52] Oswald J. Smith, *The Work God Blesses*. Marshall, 1955, 45.

[53] Oswald J. Smith, *The Work God Blesses*. Marshall, 1955, 65.

[54] Isaiah 66

[55] James 5:7-8 ESV

[56] "Parts of the Seed." *AgEdLibrary.com*, CAERT, Inc. , 2006, www.mycaert.com/samples/070026.pdf.

[57] Mark 4:26-28 NIV

[58] Mark 4:30-32 NIV

[59] Joel Salatin, *The Marvelous Pigness of Pigs: Respecting and Caring for All God's Creation* (New York, NY: Faithwords, 2017), p. 45.

[60] 2 Timothy 3:5 NIV

[61] Kyle Idleman, *AHA: Awakening, Honesty, Action: the God Moment That Changes Everything* (Colorado Springs, CO: David C Cook), 2014, 86.

[62] Ephesians 2:8-10 NIV

[63] Romans 5:8 NIV

[64] 2 Corinthians 9:6 NIV

[65] Matthew 7:15-20

[66] Michael Green, "The Message of Matthew," in *Tyndale Commentary*, ed. Leon Morris (Illinois: Intervarsity Press, 1987), 109.

[67] Galatians 5:22-23 NIV

[68] Nikki Tilley, "What Makes Plants Grow: Plants Growing Needs," *Gardening Know How*, www.gardeningknowhow.com/.

[69] Ephesians 5:16-17 NIV

[70] Proverbs 18:21 NIV

[71] James 3:5-6 NIV

[72] 1 Corinthians 6:19-20

[73] W.P. Armstrong, "Blowing In The Wind: Seeds and Fruits Dispersed by Wind," *Wayne's Word*, 1995, www2.palomar.edu/users/warmstrong/plfeb99.htm.

[74] Ecclesiastes 3:11 ESV

[75] 1 Peter 1:23-25 ESV

[76] Donald Bickelhaupt, "Soil PH: What It Means," *Around*

Your World , SUNY College of Environmental Science and Forestry, www.esf.edu/pubprog/brochure/soilph/soilph.htm.

[77] Isaiah 50:4a KJV

[78] Proverbs 25:11 ESV

[79] Romans 12:15 NIV

[80] Anonymous

[81] "Environment," *Merriam-Webster*, www.merriam-webster.com/dictionary/environment.

[82] Starr, Michelle. "New Research Shows Most Human Pregnancies End in Miscarriage." *ScienceAlert*, 1 Aug. 2018, www.sciencealert.com/meta-analysis-finds-majority-of-human-pregnancies-end-in-miscarriage-biorxiv.

[83] Robert Lamb, "What Is It about Earth That Makes It Just Right for Life?" *HowStuffWorks Science*, HowStuffWorks, 28 June 2018, science.howstuffworks.com/life/evolution/earth-just-right-for-life.htm.

[84] 1 Peter 2:12 NIV

[85] Matthew 5:13 NIV

[86] Matthew 5:14-16 NIV

[87] Isaiah 29:13 NIV

[88] John 8:12 NIV

[89] John 1:4-5 NIV

[90] 1 Timothy 2:3-4 NIV

[91] Matthew 6:10 NIV

[92] John 4:10 NIV

[93] John 4:13-14 NIV

[94] John 10:10 NIV
[95] Mark 4:4 NIV
[96] Mark 4:14-15 NIV
[97] 1 John 4:4 NIV
[98] 1 Corinthians 2:16 NIV
[99] 2 Corinthians 10:4 NIV
[100] 2 Corinthians 3:4-6 AMP
[101] Mark 10:47
[102] Mark 10:49 ESV
[103] Mark 10:51 ESV
[104] Isaiah 60:1-3 ESV
[105] Luke 10:2 NIV
[106] Romans 1:13 NIV
[107] Galatians 6:9 NIV

Made in the USA
Middletown, DE
28 January 2019